1 14 + 25 = _____

2

28	280	208
+21	+210	+201

3 Write everything you know about what makes a figure a square.

_____

_____

_____

_____

4 What are 10 tens equal to?

5 Ben has sixty-seven marbles. If he gives thirteen of them away, how many will he have left?

_____ marbles

Show your work.

Daily Math Practice

1 52 – 41 = _____

2 Use the number line to solve the problems.

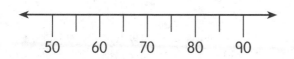

65	75	85
– 15	– 15	– 15

3 Which polygon has six sides?

○ pentagon   ○ trapezoid

○ hexagon   ○ octagon

4

+

$\frac{1}{7} + \frac{1}{7} =$ _____

5 Jimmy and Alex each collect baseball cards. Together, they have 128 cards. If Jimmy has 72 cards, how many does Alex have?

_____ cards

1   2 × 9 = _____

2   5   50
     × 8   × 8
    ‾‾‾   ‾‾‾

3   Which measurement is the longest?

   ○ 2 yards

   ○ $7\frac{1}{2}$ feet

   ○ 83 inches

4   Write the place and the value of **4** in each number.

   943   _____   _____

   4,093   _____   _____

5   Sally walks past 16 houses on her way to school. If each house has two dogs, how many dogs does Sally pass as she walks to school?

        _____ dogs

   Show your work.

1   28 ÷ 4 = _____

2   3)‾12‾   4)‾12‾

3   Write the correct symbol in the circle.

       <   =   >

   45 ◯ 29   37 ◯ 68

   81 ◯ 90   74 ◯ 47

4   Write the next three numbers in the pattern.

   7   12   17   22   _____   _____   _____

5   Jennifer wants to buy two new CDs. Each CD costs $14.00. If she has $9.00, how much more money does she need?

        $_____

   Show your work.

➤ **Activity 1**

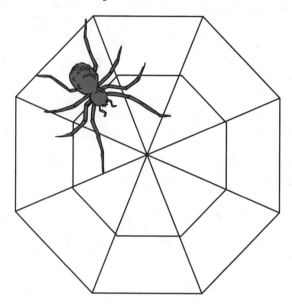

1. What shape is the spider's web?

   _____

2. How many triangles are in the web?

   _____ triangles

3. What other shape do you see in the web?

   _____

   How many?   _____

➤ **Activity 2**

How many facts can you solve in one minute?

6 x 2	3 x 7	8 x 4	5 x 9	11 x 1	2 x 0	12 x 10	9 x 8
3 x 4	11 x 12	7 x 5	1 x 2	0 x 6	10 x 9	8 x 6	7 x 4

7)77	9)54	5)20	8)64	6)72	3)12	2)16	12)84
10)50	1)4	8)96	3)18	9)27	7)63	4)36	11)132

_____ correct

1 41 + 39 = _____

2
55	65	75
+19	+18	+17

3 Write the correct symbol in the circle.
Hint: 12 inches = 1 foot; 3 feet = 1 yard

    <   =   >

5 feet ◯ 60 inches

9 feet ◯ 4 yards

4 What will the temperature be if it increases 13°?

_____

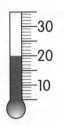

5 Cathy is two years older than Wendy. Wendy is eight years old. How old will Cathy be in two years?

_____ years old

Show your work.

1 26 − 12 = _____

2
49	49	49
− 5	−15	−25

3

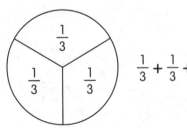

$\frac{1}{3} + \frac{1}{3} + \frac{1}{3} =$ _____

4 Round to the nearest hundred.

369 _____   826 _____

5 To earn money, Greg and Juan collected newspapers to recycle. They agreed to split all the money they made. The first day, Greg was paid $2.00 for his papers, and Juan got $1.50 for his. The next day, Greg made $1.75, and Juan made $3.25. Dividing all the money equally, how much did each boy receive?

$_____

1 90 x 5 = _____

2
```
   4        450
 x 1      x   1
---        ---
```

3 Name the solid figure that has congruent squares on all six sides.

_____

Draw the figure.

4 What fraction of the figure is shaded?

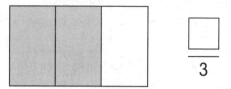

$$\frac{}{3}$$

5 Vanessa, Emma, and Marta went to the beach to collect seashells. Vanessa found 14 shells, Emma found 16 shells, and Marta collected 20 shells. How many shells did the girls collect altogether?

_____ shells

1 42 ÷ 6 = _____

2 7)63   9)63

3 Find the perimeter.

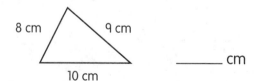

_____ cm

4 Circle all the numbers that are factors of **8**.

1   2   3   4   5   6   7   8

5 Ivan likes ice-cream cones. At the ice-cream parlor, a single-scoop cone costs 75¢. Each additional scoop of ice cream costs 50¢. Ivan earns 25¢ each time he takes out the trash. How many times will he have to take out the trash to buy a double-scoop cone?

_____ times

➤ **Activity 1**

Make a bar graph on the grid to show the information in the table below.

Drinks	Number of Students
soda	16
milk	8
water	10
juice	5

➤ **Activity 2**

Louisa and two friends decided to make a pizza for lunch. They wanted to share the pizza evenly but wondered about whether to use a rectangular pan or a circular pan and how many pieces to cut. The shapes below show what each girl suggested. Color Louisa's share of each pizza.

A 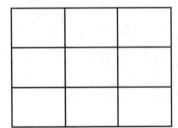   B 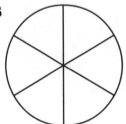   C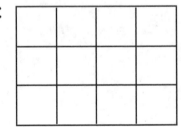

1. Write Louisa's share of each pizza as a fraction. A _____ B _____ C _____

2. Write each fraction above in simplest form. A _____ B _____ C _____

1   53 + 74 = _____

2
```
  36        37        38
 +62       +63       +64
____      ____      ____
```

3   How many blocks are in the figure?

    ○ 24

    ○ 28

    ○ 36

4   Is 1,076 odd or even? _____

5   Antonio can ride his bike from his house to school in 7 minutes, from school to DJ's house in 4 minutes, from DJ's house to the mall in 6 minutes, and from the mall to his house in 3 minutes. If Antonio leaves school at 3:30 p.m., rides past DJ's, and stops at the mall for 20 minutes to have some frozen yogurt, at what time will he get home?

    ○ 4:00   ○ 4:03   ○ 4:05

1   58 – 37 = _____

2
```
   63        630       6,300
  -41       -410      -4,100
____      ____      _____
```

3   Which activity does Kim spend the least amount of time doing?

☐ Sleeping
▨ School
◼ Meals
▤ Homework
◼ Chores

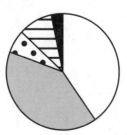

_____

4   Which container holds more water?

    ○ 8-ounce measuring cup

    ○ one-pint jar

5   Kristie wants to treat some friends to a movie. Tickets for the early show cost $2.50 each. For later shows, tickets cost $4.00 each. If Kristie's mom gives her $20.00, how many more friends can Kristie take with her to the early show than to a later show?

    ○ 3   ○ 4   ○ 5

1 710 x 0 = _____

2
```
  12        12
x  5       x10
```

3 Draw an **X** on the figure if it is **not** a trapezoid.

4 Draw the next figure in the pattern.

5 Yolanda's dog had six puppies. After choosing one puppy for herself, Yolanda decided to sell the rest of the puppies for thirty dollars each. How much money will Yolanda make if she sells all the remaining puppies?

$_____

1 48 ÷ 8 = _____

2 22)$\overline{44}$ 222)$\overline{444}$

3 Find the area.

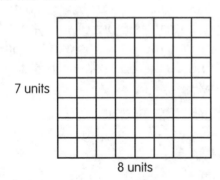

7 units

8 units

_____ square units

4 Circle the larger number.

0.8   2.0

5 Marco is 4 feet tall. His younger brother Carlos is 7 inches shorter. Marco's older brother Raul is 13 inches taller than Carlos. How tall is Raul?

_____ feet   _____ inches

Read the rules.

Rules (for 2 players)

- Take turns spinning the spinner.
- If the arrow lands on white, the player who spins gets a point.
- If the arrow lands on gray, the other player gets a point.
- The first player to get 20 points wins the game.

Look at the spinners.

A
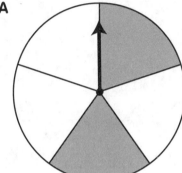

B
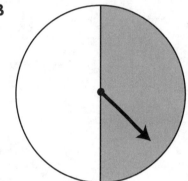

C
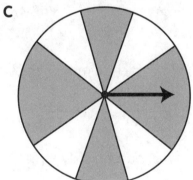

D
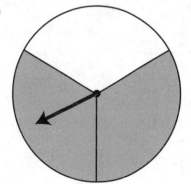

Which spinner will make the game fair? _____

Explain your choice.

_____

_____

_____

_____

1 302 + 586 = _____

2
```
  212        312        512
+ 410      + 310      + 110
```

3 What is the ratio of shaded boxes to the total number of boxes? Write the answer as a fraction.

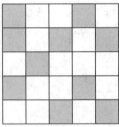 _____

4 Round to the tens place to estimate the product of 11 times 351.

_____

5 Kevin has 28 marbles. Half of his marbles are green, 3 are red, 4 are blue, and the rest are white. How many white marbles does Kevin have?

_____ white marbles

1 365 − 143 = _____

2
```
  855        855        855
− 745      − 746      − 756
```

3 Shade the squares to show the equation. Write the answer on the line.

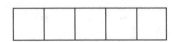

$\frac{1}{5} + \frac{1}{5} + \frac{1}{5} + \frac{1}{5} =$ _____

4 Write each number in standard form.

two hundred sixty-three   _____

two thousand sixty-three   _____

5 Sylvia has three pet gerbils. If two of her gerbils each have six babies every two months, how many babies will the gerbils have altogether over one year's time?

_____ babies

1 $33 \times 6 =$ _____

2 $\begin{array}{r} 60 \\ \times\ 4 \\ \hline \end{array}$ $\begin{array}{r} 600 \\ \times\ 4 \\ \hline \end{array}$ $\begin{array}{r} 6{,}000 \\ \times\ 4 \\ \hline \end{array}$

3   Fill in 0.1 of the set.

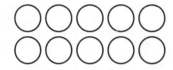

What is another way to write 0.1? _____

4   If $n = 2$, then $n + 93 =$ _____.

5   The gas tank of Ted's car holds 12 gallons. The car can go 20 miles on each gallon of gas. If Ted starts a 750-mile trip with a full tank of gas, what is the minimum number of times that he will need to stop for more gas?

_____ times

1 $1{,}055 \div 5 =$ _____

2 $20\overline{)180}$ $18\overline{)200}$

3   How many unit blocks are in the figure?

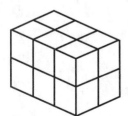

_____ unit blocks

4 $\frac{1}{8} + \frac{2}{8} + \frac{3}{8} =$ _____

5   Andrea owns 27 video games, and she has played them all many times. A new store in town will trade three used games for a new one. If Andrea trades in $\frac{1}{3}$ of her current games, how many new games can she get?

_____ games

1. The Venn diagram below shows products, or multiples, less than **50** for the numbers **5** and **4**. The center section of the diagram is where the common multiples should be written. Fill in the common multiples to complete the diagram.

Multiples of 5 and 4

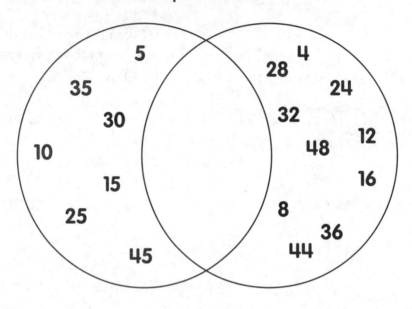

2. Complete the Venn diagram below to show all the multiples and common multiples less than **40** for the numbers **3** and **4**.

Multiples of 3 and 4

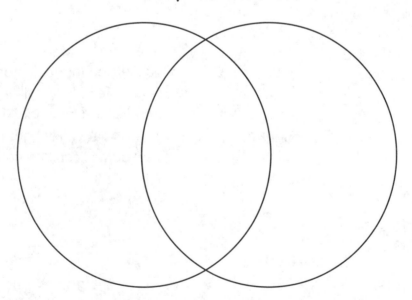

1 165 + 881 = _____

2
```
  638        439
 +347       +276
```

3 How many different ways can 3 kids line up for lunch?

_____ ways

Use the numbers **1**, **2**, and **3** to show each different way.

4 How long is the rocket?

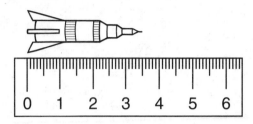

_____ cm   _____ mm

5 Kent caught an 8 pound 3 ounce trout in Pike Lake. The season's record catch so far is 129 ounces. Did Kent's fish beat the record?

○ **yes**   ○ **no**

1 458 − 129 = _____

2
```
  742        921
 −157       −830
```

3 What are the coordinates of **X** on the grid?

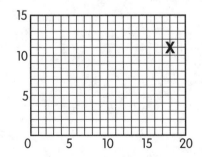

_____

4 What is the inverse of addition?

○ division
○ subtraction
○ multiplication

5 Jody has saved $12.85 to buy a new DVD. If the DVD costs $34.50, how much more does Jody have to save?

$_____

1 210 x 7 = _____

2
```
    8        38
  x 8       x 8
  ___       ___
```

3 Write the decimal that names the shaded part. Then write the fraction form of the decimal.

decimal _____   fraction _____

4 List the first four multiples of 4.

_____ _____ _____ _____

5 When Bill and Josh exchanged phone numbers, they realized that their numbers both have the same digits in them. The digits are **5**, **3**, **7**, **9**, **7**, **8**, and **2**. Bill's phone number is the smallest number that can be created with these digits. Josh's phone number is the largest number. What are their phone numbers?

Bill _____

Josh _____

1 729 ÷ 8 = _____

2 7)7   7)77   7)777

3 Write the correct symbol in the circle.

< = >

4.0 ◯ 0.4

0.4 ◯ 0.40

4 Follow the rule **x2 +2** to complete the pattern.

8 _____ _____ _____ _____ _____

5 Ian started playing a video game at 3:45 p.m. and played for 2 hours and 25 minutes straight. At what time did he stop playing?

_____

Make a bar graph to show the data on the tally chart. (Remember to include axis labels and a title on your graph.)

Summer Super-Readers	
Name	Number of Books
Tyler	卌 III
Nate	卌
Cherié	卌 I
Max	卌 卌
Shayla	卌 卌 II
Hamid	卌 I
Kelly	卌 卌

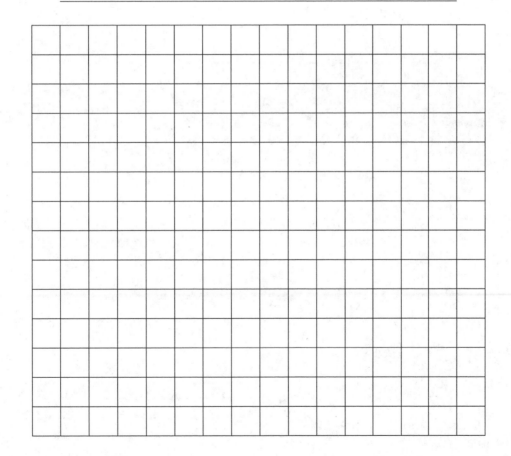

1 467 + 232 = _____

2
```
  584        698
+ 392      + 475
-----      -----
```

3 Calculate the perimeter (**p**) and the area (**a**) of the figure if each square measures 1 inch by 1 inch.

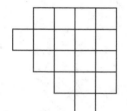

p = _____

a = _____

4 What shape has 8 sides and 8 angles?

_____

5 Brandon has a stack of books on his desk. The first book has 10 pages. The second book has twice as many pages. The third book has 40 pages, which is twice as many pages as the second book. If this pattern continues, how many pages will the eighth book have?

_____ pages

1 197 – 126 = _____

2
```
  738        412
– 295      – 267
-----      -----
```

3 Which circle shows $\frac{2}{3}$ shaded? _____

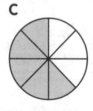

A   B   C

4 Write the correct symbol in the circle.

< = >

6 quarts ◯ $\frac{1}{2}$ gallon

10 ounces ◯ 2 cups

1 gallon ◯ 8 pints

5 Abby is half as old as her dad, and twice as old as her brother. If her brother is 9 years old, how old is her dad?

_____ years old

1 2 x 3 x 4 = _____

2
```
  27        26
x  6      x  7
```

3 Complete the function table to show $3\frac{1}{3}$ cups of flour per pound.

pounds	2	3	5	7
cups				

4 Draw all possible lines of symmetry.

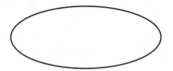

5 Rafael can run 2 miles in 16 minutes. At this rate, how long will it take him to run 5 miles?

_____ minutes

1 275 ÷ 5 = _____

2 3)‾1‾8‾0   6)‾1‾8‾0   9)‾1‾8‾0

3 What figure comes next in the pattern?

 _____

4 What are 20 tens equal to? _____

5 Maria is selling T-shirts to raise money for her school's student council. Each shirt sells for $8.00, and half of the money goes to the student council. If Maria sells 12 shirts, how much money will go to the student council?

$_____

➤ **Activity 1**

Write **acute**, **obtuse**, or **right** on the line to name each angle.

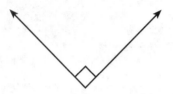

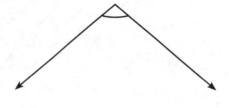

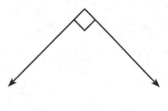

_____

_____

_____

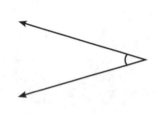

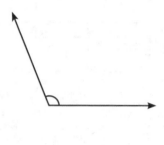

_____

_____

_____

➤ **Activity 2**

Round the numbers in each column to the place indicated.

tens	hundreds	thousands
712 _____	635 _____	4,639 _____
254 _____	481 _____	6,060 _____
908 _____	549 _____	3,951 _____
399 _____	1,972 _____	12,645 _____
157 _____	5,460 _____	47,098 _____
845 _____	2,028 _____	19,725 _____

1 4,719 + 5,260 = _____

2
$8\frac{2}{6}$ $10\frac{5}{6}$
$+2\frac{5}{6}$ $-3\frac{2}{6}$

3 Circle the digit that is in the thousands place.

26,195

4 Circle the letter that represents **4** on the number line.

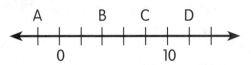

5 Sarah and Rico both collect rocks. If Sarah has three times as many rocks as Rico, and she has 84 rocks, how many rocks does Rico have?

_____ rocks

Show your work.

1 6,328 − 5,104 = _____

2 6)49   10)71

3 Write the correct symbol in the circle.

< = >

24.36 ◯ 243.6

4.362 ◯ 4.632

0.5 ◯ 0.500

4 Which units measure weight?

◯ liters   ◯ pints
◯ yards   ◯ ounces
◯ kilograms   ◯ kilometers

5 Tim has a 10-gallon fish tank in his bedroom. In it, he has 15 neon tetras, 38 guppies, and 3 rainbow fish. How many fish does Tim have in all?

_____ fish

1 21 × 40 = _____

2
```
  100        10        110
×   7      ×  7      ×   7
```

3 How many sides does each polygon have?

octagon _____

hexagon _____

pentagon _____

4 Round 275,390 to the nearest ten thousand.

_____

5 Jose built the pyramid of blocks below, but he wants to make it bigger. If he makes the pyramid seven rows high, how many blocks would be in the bottom row?

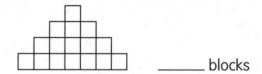 _____ blocks

1 400 ÷ 10 = _____

2 5)40   5)400   5)440

3 How many of each unit are in a gallon?

_____ pints = 1 gallon

_____ quarts = 1 gallon

_____ cups = 1 gallon

4 If $\frac{1}{5} + \frac{1}{5} + \frac{1}{5} = \frac{3}{5}$, then $\frac{1}{5} \times$ _____ $= \frac{3}{5}$.

5 Matt has 2 pet mice. Eric has 3 pet birds. Kyle has 4 pet hamsters. If each pet eats $\frac{1}{4}$ cup of food each day, how much food altogether will the boys' pets eat in 8 days?

_____ cups of food

Show your work.

If you take four squares that are each 1 unit by 1 unit in size and join them side by side in a straight line, you will have a figure with a perimeter of 10 units and an area of 4 square units.

perimeter = 10 units

area = 4 square units

In the boxes below, show four more ways to arrange the squares. They have to be joined along an edge and not just at a corner. Write the perimeter and the area of each figure you create.

perimeter = _____ units **area** = _____ square units	**perimeter** = _____ units **area** = _____ square units
perimeter = _____ units **area** = _____ square units	**perimeter** = _____ units **area** = _____ square units

1 3,857 + 2,691 = _____

2
```
  7,243          8,852
+ 1,609        − 7,243
```

3 How many?

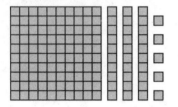

_____

4 Draw the missing figures in the empty boxes.

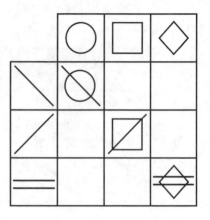

5 Min is twice as tall as her brother. If Min is 5 feet 3 inches tall, how tall is her brother?

_____ feet _____ inches

1 6,842 − 5,963 = _____

2
```
   93             93
 ×  3           × 30
```

3 Circle all the numbers that are factors of **10**.

1   2   3   4   5   6

10   15   20   25   30   35

50   60   70   80   90   100

4 Write 56,902 in expanded form.

_____

5 Diego tries not to step on any cracks in the sidewalk. On his way home from school, he walks past 12 houses. There are 15 cracks on the sidewalk in front of each house. How many cracks in all does Diego have to step over when he walks home from school?

_____ cracks

1 52 × 10 = _____

2   6   20   26
     × 3   × 3   × 3
   ____   ____   ____

3 Write the fraction that names the shaded part in simplest form.

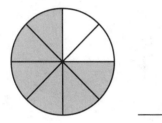

_____

4 Is 8,461 an odd or an even number?

_____

5 Lily's grandmother gave her 15 china dolls. If Lily gives one-third of them to her sister Nina, how many dolls will Nina have?

_____ dolls

1 2,268 − 1,359 = _____

2 2)30   2)6   2)306

3 What is the name of a polygon with five sides?

_____

Draw the shape.

4 Write the correct symbol in the circle.

< = >

212,594 ◯ 221,495

1,910,989 ◯ 1,911,203

5 Todd is walking dogs to earn money. He is trying to earn $15.00. If he gets paid $2.50 per dog, how many dogs will Todd have to walk?

_____ dogs

Look at the graph and then mark the statements that are true.

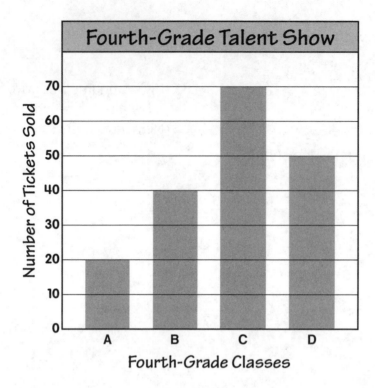

Fourth-Grade Talent Show

Number of Tickets Sold

Fourth-Grade Classes

○ Class C sold the most tickets.

○ Class A sold half as many tickets as Class D.

○ Class C sold $2\frac{1}{2}$ times more tickets than Class A.

○ Class B sold $\frac{1}{5}$ fewer tickets than Class D.

○ Classes A and B together sold $\frac{1}{5}$ as many tickets as Class C.

○ Classes A and C together sold as many tickets as
Classes B and D together.

1 4,751 + 3,926 = _____

2
49
x 10

49
x 2

49
x 12

3 Is **4** a good estimate for **158 ÷ 41**?

○ **yes**   ○ **no**

Tell why or why not.

_____

_____

_____

4 List the first five multiples of 5.

_____ _____ _____ _____ _____

5 Jesse wanted a stamp collection. His grandfather gave him 48 stamps to start it. Then his parents gave him 23 stamps, and his aunt gave him 17 stamps. How many stamps does Jesse have in his collection?

_____ stamps

1 6,472 – 5,439 = _____

2 10)800   10)8,000

3 The clock shows the time that Kim's party ended. If the party lasted 2 hours and 45 minutes, at what time did it start?

_____

4 Write the number one million seventy-four.

_____

5 Sharon can buy a candy bar from the grocery store for $1.19, while the gas station sells candy bars at 3 for $4.00, and the drugstore sells a package of six for $6.99. Which place has the best price?

○ grocery store
○ gas station
○ drugstore

1 118 × 4 = _____

2
```
  2,754
+   368
_____
```
```
         _____
        – 2,754
            368
```

3 Draw an **X** on the figures that are **not** polygons.

4 If $a = 50$, then $a - 37 =$ _____.

5 Trevor is racing his dirt bike at about 30 miles per hour. If he keeps up this rate for an hour and a half, how many miles will he travel?

_____ miles

Show your work.

1 775 ÷ 5 = _____

2 $\frac{10}{11} - \frac{3}{11} =$ _____ $\frac{7}{8} - \frac{4}{8} =$ _____

3 What is the volume?

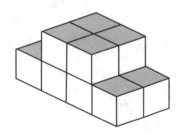

_____ cubic units

4 Write the correct symbol in the circle.

< = >

8 centimeters ⟡ 8 millimeters

5 decimeters ⟡ 5 meters

10 kilometers ⟡ 10,000 meters

5 Cindy is buying food for her pet parrot. If the price of birdseed is $3.48 a bag, and Cindy buys five bags, how much will the birdseed cost?

$_____

At 11:11, the digits on a digital clock are all the same. The time 11:11 can also be read in reverse order and still be 11:11.

1. At what other times are the digits on a digital clock all the same?
   Write your answers on the clocks. (**Hint:** There may be more clocks than you need.)

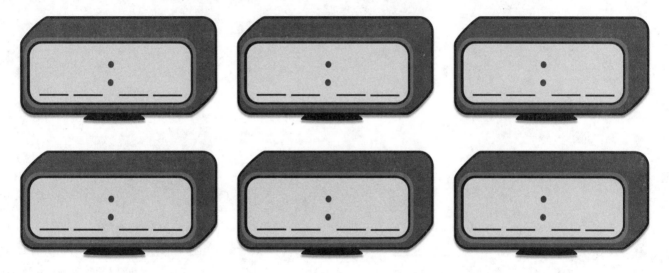

2. At what other times can the digits on a digital clock be read in reverse order?
   (Be careful! The time 9:09 doesn't work because the colon would be in the wrong place. The reverse order of 9:09 would be 90:9.)

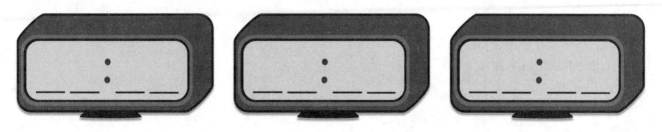

1 187 + 247 + 317 = _____

2 27,954
    +   368

3 Write each fraction in simplest form.

$\frac{2}{8}$ = _____ $\frac{5}{10}$ = _____

$\frac{4}{6}$ = _____ $\frac{8}{12}$ = _____

$\frac{12}{16}$ = _____ $\frac{21}{24}$ = _____

4 What is the inverse of 50 x 10 = 500?

_____

5 Ben jogs with his father every morning. On Saturdays and Sundays, they run 4 miles. On all other days they run 2 miles. How many miles does Ben run each week?

_____ miles

1 36,978 – 12,045 = _____

2   52   52   52
    x 10   x 11   x 12

3 How many lines of symmetry does the figure have? _____
Draw them.

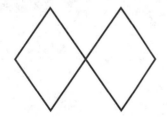

4 Ramon has nine quarters, thirteen dimes, six nickels, and seven pennies. How much money does he have?

$_____

5 Jenny can type 30 words per minute. How many words can she type in 25 minutes?

_____ words

1 19 × 60 = _____

2 714 + 714 + 714 = _____

   714 × 3 = _____

3 Hallie is helping put away dishes in the school cafeteria. She is stacking bowls to put into the cupboard. If she has 62 bowls and can put a maximum of 4 bowls in each stack, what is the minimum number of stacks Hallie will have?

   _____ stacks

4 Plot the point (5, 12) on the grid.

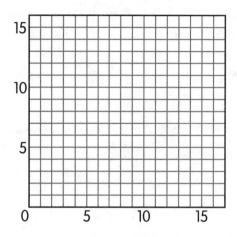

5 Which is heavier, one pound of rocks or one pound of feathers?

   _____

1 114 ÷ 7 = _____

2 $2\overline{)428}$ $4\overline{)428}$

3 How many different outfits can Amy make with 3 blouses and 3 pairs of pants?

   _____ outfits

   Show your work.

4 Add $\frac{11}{12}$ and $\frac{7}{12}$ and write the answer in simplest form.

   _____

   Show your work.

5 Mario is going to an amusement park on Saturday. The park charges $1.50 per ride, and Mario wants to go on all 19 rides at least once. What is the least amount of money he will need?

   $_____

➤ Activity 1

Brian is thinking of a number and gives the following clues. Use the number chart to help you figure out Brian's number.

Clues

- It is less than 50.
- It is greater than 20.
- It is **not** a multiple of 5.
- It is an odd number.
- It has a 3 in the ones place.
- It is **not** a prime number.

Number Chart									
1	2	3	4	5	6	7	8	9	10
11	12	13	14	15	16	17	18	19	20
21	22	23	24	25	26	27	28	29	30
31	32	33	34	35	36	37	38	39	40
41	42	43	44	45	46	47	48	49	50
51	52	53	54	55	56	57	58	59	60

What is the number Brian is thinking of? _____

➤ Activity 2

Fill in the missing integers on each number line.

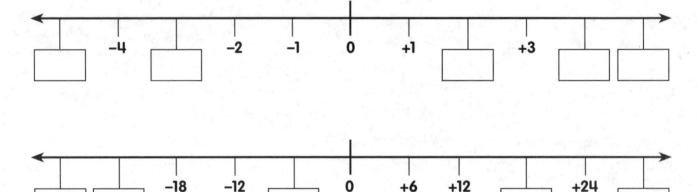

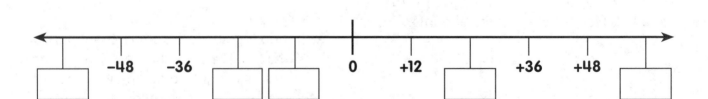

1 4,725 + 3,626 = _____

2 $4\frac{3}{8}$ ☐

   $+ 3\frac{4}{8}$ $- 3\frac{4}{8}$
   _____   _____
   ☐ $4\frac{3}{8}$

3 Which number is 7,918 rounded to the greatest place?

   ○ 7,900   ○ 7,920   ○ 8,000

4 Continue the pattern.

   35 49 63 77 _____ _____ _____

5 Holly reached into her pocket and pulled out nine coins that equaled 33¢. What two different combinations of coins could she have had?

   _____

   _____

1 7,109 – 5,423 = _____

2   16   106
   x 7   x 7

3 What is the perimeter of the figure if each square is 1 inch by 1 inch?

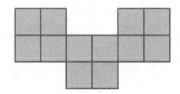

   _____

4 Write each decimal as a fraction.

   0.3 _____   0.03 _____   0.003 _____

5 Jason has three times as many chickens as he has dogs. If he has 18 chickens, how many dogs does he have?

   _____ dogs

1   550 ÷ 7 = _____

2   72   72
    x 9   x 29

3   Which item has the shape of a cylinder?

   ○ pencil
   ○ baseball
   ○ book

4   Write the fraction for the shaded part of the figure in decimal form.

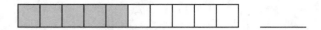   _____

5   This soccer season, Rosa scored at least one goal during half of all the games she played in. If Rosa played in eight games, during how many games did she score a goal?

      _____ games

1   567 ÷ 3 = _____

2   9)459   9)495

3   Circle all the prime numbers.

     1   2   3   4   5

     6   7   8   9   10

4   If 100 x 10 = 1,000, then 1,000 ÷ 100 = _____.

5   April is making muffins for a bake sale. She has 8 boxes of muffin mix, and each box makes a dozen muffins. How many muffins can April make for the bake sale?

      _____ muffins

Which figure below shows what this
building would look like from the opposite
side (looking at it from where the
arrow is pointing)?

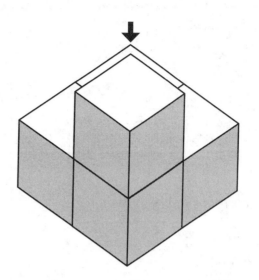

_____

A

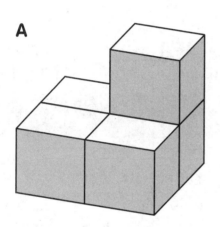

B

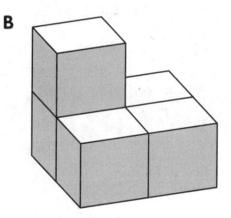

C

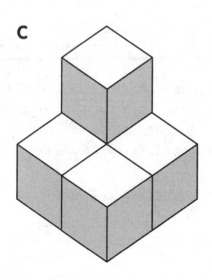

D

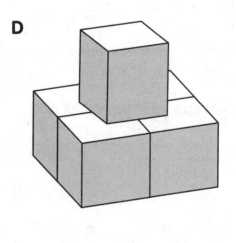

1. $\frac{5}{8} + \frac{7}{8} + \frac{3}{8} =$ _____

2. 23,846
   + 5,152

3. Write the correct symbol in the circle.

   < = >

   2 cups ◯ 1 quart

   4 cups ◯ 1 quart

   8 cups ◯ 1 pint

4. Draw an **X** on the number line to show **2.7**.

5. Sam is playing with four friends in his backyard. They are jumping on Sam's trampoline, but the trampoline will hold only two people at a time. If each friend wants to jump with each of the others, how many times in all does each pair of friends have to jump?

   _____ times

1. $\frac{9}{10} - \frac{6}{10} =$ _____

2. 29,496
   − 17,391

3. Round each decimal to the tenths place.

   3.08 _____

   5.35 _____

   8.43 _____

4. List all the factors of 19.

   _____

5. Susan is a bird-watcher. She saw 3 beautiful birds on Monday. On Tuesday, she saw 4 more. On Wednesday, she saw 6, but on Thursday, she didn't see any. Then on Friday, she saw 4 again. Assuming that each bird sighting was a different bird, how many birds did Susan see during the week?

   _____ birds

1   61 x 20 = _____

2   416   8)416
    x   8

3   Is 27 a prime number?

    ◯ **yes**   ◯ **no**

    Tell why or why not.

    _____

    _____

    _____

4   Draw the next figure in the pattern.

    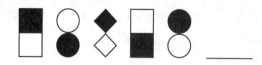 _____

5   Kani's desk has three drawers in it. In each drawer, Kani has 12 puzzles, and each puzzle has 100 pieces. How many puzzle pieces does Kani have in all?

    _____ puzzle pieces

1   639 ÷ 9 = _____

2   3)3,120   6)2,310

3   What are the perimeter (**p**) and the area (**a**) of the figure if each square is 1 inch by 1 inch?

    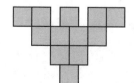

    p = _____

    a = _____

4   There are 8 boys and 9 girls in Mr. Chen's classroom. What is the ratio of boys to girls?

    ◯ 8:9   ◯ 9:8

5   Sydney was collecting aluminum cans to recycle. She picked up 5 bags of cans from her next-door neighbor and twice as many from each of two neighbors across the street. How many bags of cans did Sydney have in all?

    _____ bags of cans

➤ **Activity 1**

1. Write the number pattern shown by the squares below.   _____ _____ _____ _____

 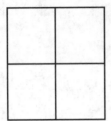 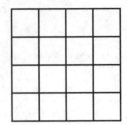 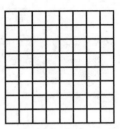

2. What is the rule for the pattern?   _____

3. If you continue the pattern, what would the next two numbers be?   _____ _____

➤ **Activity 2**

1. If 12 inches = 1 foot, then 18 inches = _____ feet.

2. If 8 ounces = 1 cup, then 24 ounces = _____ cups.

3. If 16 ounces = 1 pound, then 80 ounces = _____ pounds.

4. If 100 centimeters = 1 meter, then 600 centimeters = _____ meters.

5. If 1,000 milligrams = 1 gram, then 500 milligrams = _____ gram.

6. If 30 minutes = $\frac{1}{2}$ hour, then 180 minutes = _____ hours.

7. If 20 nickels = $1.00, then 50 nickels = $_____.

8. If ♦ = 5 people, then ♦♦♦♦♦♦♦ = _____ people.

1. 31.54 + 56.15 = _____

2.
```
  568        685
+ 239      + 329
```

3. Mark the place that **5** has in the number 53,890.

   ○ thousands

   ○ ten thousands

   ○ hundreds

4. How many feet are in 9 yards?

   _____ feet

5. If you set the pyramid below on top of the cube, how many faces will the new figure have?

   _____ faces

1. 3,684 – 1,792 = _____

2.
```
   85.70
 – 10.42
 [      ]
```
```
 [        ]
 + 10.42
   85.70
```

3. Write each number in standard form.

   three hundred thirty-three _____

   three thousand thirty-three _____

   thirty thousand thirty-three _____

4. How many eggs are there in half of three dozen?

   _____ eggs

5. Mara's necklace has 26 fewer beads than her sister Carla's. If Carla's necklace has 123 beads, how many beads does Mara's necklace have?

   _____ beads

   Show your work.

1   103 × 9 = _____

2
$$\begin{array}{ccc} 12 & 12 & 12 \\ \times\ 8 & \times 10 & \times 18 \end{array}$$

$\boxed{} + \boxed{} = \boxed{}$

3   Which kind of triangle has two sides that are the same length?

○ isosceles

○ equilateral

○ scalene

4   If $w = 17$, then $w \times 3 =$ _____.

5   Tara likes to draw pictures on the back of her homework papers. It takes her about 5 minutes to draw each picture. This week, she turned in 18 homework assignments with pictures on them. How long did it take Tara to draw the pictures?

_____

1   288 ÷ 9 = _____

2 $8\overline{)40}$ $8\overline{)16}$ $8\overline{)4,016}$

3   Write the correct symbol in the circle.

    <   =   >

8.4 ◯ 14.0

7.2 ◯ 7.25

10.5 ◯ 9.9

4   Circle the numbers that are multiples of **3**.

   25   36   42   59

   68   73   87   91

5   Wyatt was cleaning his room and found 57 books under his bed. He stacked the books on his desk. Each stack had the same number of books in it, and no stack had fewer than 5 books. How many stacks did Wyatt make and how many books were in each stack?

_____ stacks of _____ books

Seth listed the scores on his weekly math tests for the first nine weeks of school. Make a line graph on the grid to display Seth's scores.

Week	1	2	3	4	5	6	7	8	9
Math Score	60	72	74	80	83	85	87	92	95

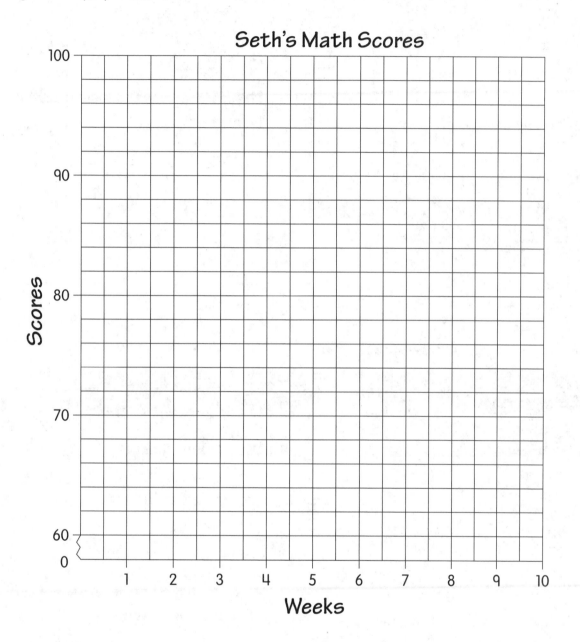

Seth's Math Scores

Which of the following conclusions can you make from the data?

○ Seth will get an **A** in math.

○ Seth's math test scores improved each week.

○ Seth's test scores went up an average of 2 points each week.

1 $7\frac{1}{3} + 9\frac{2}{3} =$ _____

2   103,251
    +   4,806
    _____

3   What kind of triangle is it?

     ○ equilateral
     ○ isosceles
     ○ scalene

4   Estimate the sum of 890 + 201.

_____

5   Nathan is saving money to buy a skateboard. The one he wants costs $124.00. He currently has $55.00. How much more does Nathan need to save?

     $_____

1   2.04 − 1.48 = _____

2   13,032
    −12,428
    _____

3   Which figure is congruent to the white shape in the box?

_____

   A   B   C   D

4   What are the first five multiples of 7?

_____ _____ _____ _____ _____

5   Julie's new puppy eats 3 cups of food each day. If the bag of dog food contains enough food for 35 days, how many cups of food are in the bag?

     _____ cups of food

Show your work.

1   181 x 4 = _____

2
```
   39          393
 x  7        x   7
```

3   Write the correct symbol in the circle.

<   =   >

$\frac{1}{4}$ ◯ 0.2

$\frac{1}{2}$ ◯ 0.5

$\frac{3}{4}$ ◯ 0.8

4   Water freezes at 32°F. What temperature is 23 degrees above freezing?

_____°F

5   Amy bought five bags of chips. Each bag cost $3.79. What was the total cost of the chips?

$_____

---

1   546 ÷ 4 = _____

2
$1\frac{1}{3}$ ☐

$+ 2\frac{1}{3}$ $- 1\frac{1}{3}$

☐ $2\frac{1}{3}$

3   Which figure is a right triangle?

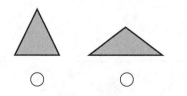

◯   ◯   ◯

4   How many pounds equal 128 ounces?

_____ pounds

5   You start out facing north. Each time you turn, you will move 90 degrees. If you turn 2 times to the right, 1 time to the left, 3 times to the right, 1 time to the left, and 2 times to the right, which way will you be facing?

◯ north   ◯ east

◯ south   ◯ west

➤ **Activity 1**

Each section of the figure below is labeled with a letter. Use the clues to find the whole number that goes in each section and what color the section should be. Write the number in each section and color the sections to show your answers.

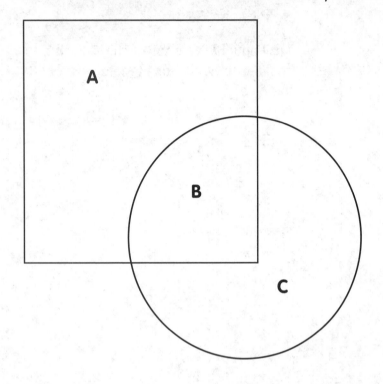

Clues

- The number in the red section is twice as much as the number in section B.

- The number in the blue section is 5.

- The smallest number is in the green section.

- The sum of the numbers in sections A and C is 13.

- The only prime number is in section A.

➤ **Activity 2**

Write each number below in expanded form.

1.   123 _____

2.   4,952 _____

3.   807 _____

4.   30,014 _____

5.   17,236 _____

6.   5,368 _____

7.   128,490 _____

8.   5,000,001 _____

1 15,400 + 679 = _____

2 10,233
    + 7,698
    ‾‾‾‾‾‾‾

3 Round each number to the tenths place.

0.95   _____

0.63   _____

0.555   _____

4 What is 3 hours and 15 minutes after 2:55 a.m.?

_____

5 Anna likes the swings at the park. She can swing back and forth 22 times per minute. If Anna swings for 15 minutes, how many times will she go back and forth?

_____ times

Show your work.

1 17.4 – 15.8 = _____

2 78,387
    –33,673
    ‾‾‾‾‾‾‾

    [   ]

    +33,673
    ‾‾‾‾‾‾‾
    78,387

3 How many dollars are 5,000 pennies worth?

$_____

Show your work.

4 Write the inverse of the problem.

12,543 – 7,213 = 5,330

_____

5 Kendall has dance lessons every Tuesday afternoon. About how many lessons does she have each month?

_____ lessons

1 31 x 70 = _____

2   522
     x   5

3 How many faces does the pyramid have?

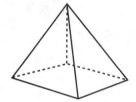

_____ faces

4 Continue the pattern.

2 4 8 10 20 _____ _____ _____

5 On week days, Aaron gets home from school at 4:30 p.m., and his bedtime is at 9:00 p.m. If he spends 90 minutes playing football, 35 minutes eating dinner, and 1 hour and 45 minutes doing homework, how much time after school will Aaron have left to play video games?

_____

1 5,621 ÷ 7 = _____

2 11)‾1‾1‾0

3 Draw the other side of the figure if the dark line represents a line of symmetry.

4 What is the perimeter of a rectangle that is 5 inches by 3 inches?

_____ inches

5 Brandon is not smiling. He just left the dentist's office, and he has 5 cavities! If it takes the dentist 14 minutes to fill one cavity, how long will it take to fill all 5 of Brandon's cavities?

_____

Make a line graph on the grid to show the information in the table. Remember to include a title, scales, and axis labels on your graph.

Month	Average High Temperature
April	63°F
May	70°F
June	76°F
July	81°F
August	84°F
September	72°F

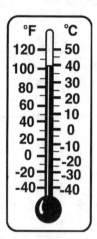

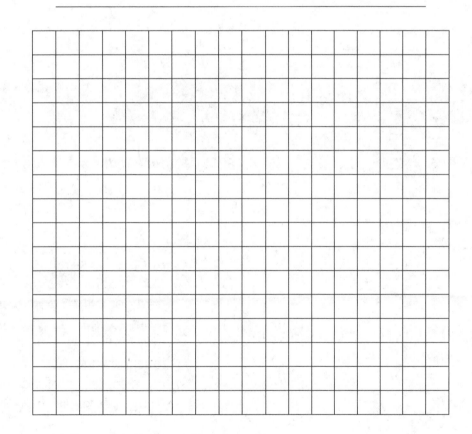

1. 24.86 + 22.23 = _____

2.
```
   349,375
 +138,452
```

3. What are the coordinates of **X**?

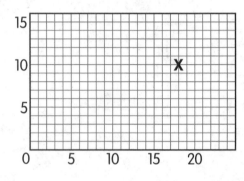

_____

4. Round 369,956 to the nearest ten thousand.

_____

5. As Shelley was doing her homework, she discovered that it takes her about 4 minutes to do each math problem. If she still has 18 problems left to do, about how long will it take her to finish her homework?

_____

1. $64\frac{5}{8} - 29\frac{3}{8} =$ _____

2.
```
   175,639
 − 39,559
```

3. What is the area of the shape if each box is 1 square centimeter?

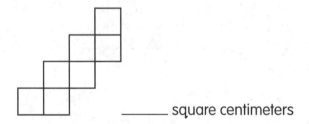

_____ square centimeters

4. How many sides does a pentagon have?

　○ 4　　○ 5　　○ 6　　○ 7

5. Andy is the kicker for his football team. During Saturday's game, he kicked three field goals for 3 points each. Then the team scored 2 touchdowns (6 points each), and Andy kicked the extra point for each touchdown (1 more point each). The other team scored a total of 20 points. Did Andy's team win the game?

　○ **yes**　　○ **no**

By how many points? _____

1 701 x 5 = _____

2   99   99
     x 9   x 90
     _____   _____

3 Fill in the circles to show $\frac{8}{12}$.

Write the fraction in simplest form. _____

4 What does ten hundred thousand equal?

_____

5 Luke went fishing and caught a trout that weighed two and a half pounds. How much did Luke's fish weigh in ounces?

_____ ounces

Show your work.

1 1,221 ÷ 3 = _____

2 6)24   6)204

3 Circle the acute angle.

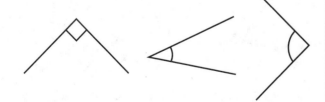

4 If $b = 7$, then 210 x b = _____.

5 Shannon is raking leaves in her yard. She figures that it will take 12 bags to hold the leaves from 2 trees. If Shannon's yard has 7 trees that are all about the same size, how many bags will she need to hold all the leaves?

_____ bags

Show your work.

➤ **Activity 1**

Triangular numbers are determined by the number of equal-sized objects arranged in the shape of an equilateral triangle. The **first** triangular number is T_1. It is represented by a single object ⬤.

The figures below are examples of the next two triangular numbers.

$$T_2 = 3 \quad \begin{array}{r} 1 \\ +2 \\ \hline 3 \end{array} \qquad T_3 = 6 \quad \begin{array}{r} 1 \\ 2 \\ +3 \\ \hline 6 \end{array}$$

Draw the figure for T_4. (**Hint:** $T_4 = 10$)

➤ **Activity 2**

How many division problems can you solve in one minute?

$2\overline{)84}$	$3\overline{)57}$	$4\overline{)68}$	$5\overline{)75}$	$6\overline{)48}$
$6\overline{)918}$	$8\overline{)584}$	$9\overline{)378}$	$7\overline{)483}$	$5\overline{)505}$
$2\overline{)2,242}$	$5\overline{)5,205}$	$7\overline{)4,935}$	$3\overline{)1,839}$	$4\overline{)9,380}$

_____ correct

1 $37\frac{1}{9} + 62\frac{5}{9} =$ _____

2 $\begin{array}{r} 308,690 \\ +\ 49,277 \\ \hline \end{array}$

3 Write the number three hundred thousand sixty-eight in expanded form.

_____

4 If 6 people want Todd Smith for class president and 17 people want Teja Johnson, what is the ratio of people wanting Todd to people wanting Teja for class president?

_____

5 Marcy was in a pie-eating contest. She was able to eat 6 cream pies that each had 15 cherries on top. How many cherries did Marcy eat?

_____ cherries

1 $63.7 - 21.4 =$ _____

2 $\begin{array}{r} 42,803 \\ -19,651 \\ \hline \end{array}$

3 Is 67 a prime number?

○ yes   ○ no

Why or why not? _____

_____

4 List all the factors of 60.

_____

5 Elizabeth was flying from Dallas to Chicago to visit her grandmother. The plane left the airport at 10:15 a.m. Lunch was served 1 hour and 42 minutes into the flight. If it took Elizabeth 23 minutes to eat, at what time did she finish her lunch?

_____

1 696 x 9 = _____

2   41
     x 13
     ―――――

3 Write the decimal for the shaded part of the circle.

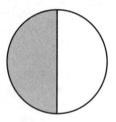

_____

4 If $x = 55$, then $x \div 11 =$ _____.

5 Brenda is half as old as her brother Bill. If Bill is 26, how old is Brenda?

_____ years old

1 309 ÷ 3 = _____

2 8)6,009

3 Continue the pattern.

☆ ☆ △ ☆ ☆ △ ☆ ____

____ ____ ____ ____

4 How many milliliters (ml) are in 1 liter?

_____ ml

5 Inga was riding on a train that had 96 cars. The train had one engine for every 24 cars. How many engines did the train have?

_____ engines

Show your work.

➤ Activity 1

Anthony has $11.80. Mark all the possible combinations of bills and coins he could have.

	$10	$5	$1	half dollar	quarter	dime	nickel	penny
○	1		1		3		1	
○		2		4		6	3	5
○			8	1	10	5	6	
○		1	6	1	1			10
○			10		3	6	5	
○	1				2	10	3	
○		1	5		6	1	2	
○		2	1		2		3	15

➤ Activity 2

An apple and a bag of pretzels from the snack machine costs a total of $1.70. The machine takes only coins in the exact amount for each item. Damien has 6 quarters and 2 dimes.

Can Damien buy both items from the machine?   ○ **yes**   ○ **no**   ○ **More information is needed.**

Explain your answer.

_____

_____

1 52,857 + 26,134 = _____

2
```
  37.5          65.42
+42.1         +78.95
```

3 Number the lengths in order from shortest to longest.

_____ 1 foot   _____ 3 feet

_____ 2 yards   _____ 18 inches

4 Write the correct symbol in the circle.

$\frac{1}{2}$ ◯ $\frac{3}{4}$

$\frac{2}{8}$ ◯ $\frac{1}{3}$

$\frac{2}{3}$ ◯ $\frac{4}{6}$

5 Dan's birthday is April 29. Beth's is 15 days later. When is Beth's birthday?

_____

1 27,293 – 11,546 = _____

2
```
  83.5          40.69
– 61.2         – 18.74
```

3 Which rule does the pattern follow?

36   72   70   140   138   276   274

◯ x2, +2

◯ x2, ÷2

◯ x2, –2

4 Draw an **X** on the number line to show **13.5**.

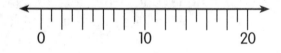

5 Cindy went to the pool to swim laps. She completed a total of 45 laps. She did 15 laps of freestyle, 12 laps of butterfly, and 10 laps of breaststroke. The rest of the laps were backstroke. How many laps of backstroke did Cindy swim?

_____ laps

1 6,310 x 6 = _____

2

45	45	45
x 10	x 1	x 11

☐ + ☐ = ☐

3 How many cubes were used to make the figure below?

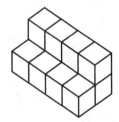

_____ cubes

4 How many different kinds of pizzas can you make if each pizza has one meat (pepperoni, sausage, or bacon) and one vegetable (mushrooms, black olives, or green peppers)?

_____ kinds of pizzas

5 Alan went horseback riding with five of his friends. They rode for three hours, and each had to pay $5.00 per hour. How much did they pay altogether?

$_____

1 1,464 ÷ 4 = _____

2 9)27   9)207   9)2,007

3 Estimate the sum of 62, 61, and 58.

_____

4 What fraction of the figure is shaded?

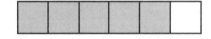

_____

5 At Taco Village, Jake ordered a taco for $1.79, a burrito for $2.79, and a soft drink for $1.19. What was the total amount of Jake's order?

$_____

➤ **Activity 1**

Write the name of each shape on the line under the correct figure.

hexagon	quadrilateral	octagon
decagon	pentagon	triangle

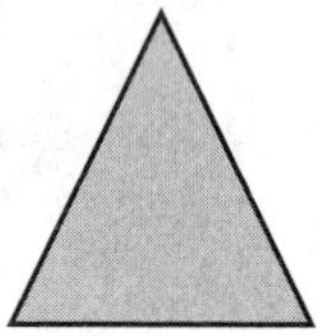

_____   _____   _____

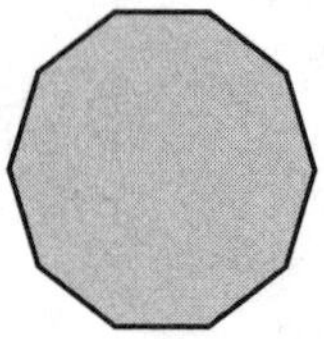

_____   _____   _____

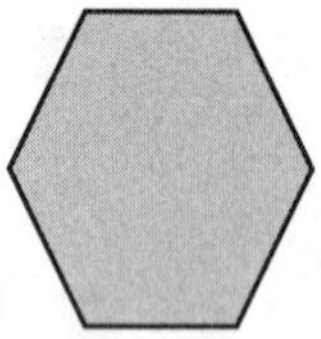

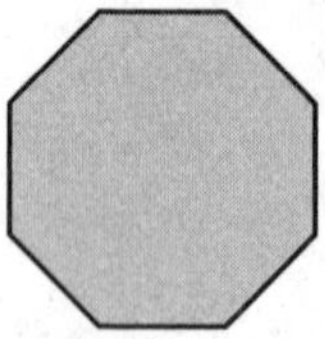

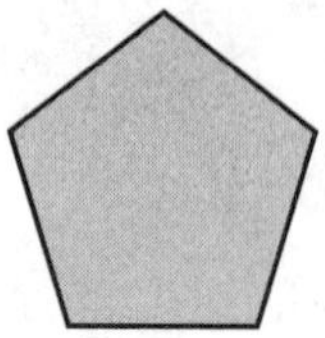

➤ **Activity 2**

Draw the lines or the figure in each box.

intersecting lines   **right triangle**   **line segment**

parallel lines   **perpendicular lines**   **parallelogram**

1 Is the equation correct?   **yes**   **no**
If **no**, correct any errors.

263.5 + 122.4 = 385.9

2 Is the equation correct?   **yes**   **no**
If **no**, correct any errors.

367 − 289 = 188

3 Write the correct symbol in the circle.

   < = >

74.29 ◯ 47.825

4 How many kilograms equal 3,000 grams?

_____ kilograms

5 Julie is stringing beads to make a necklace. She can fit nine beads on one inch of string, and she wants the necklace to be 18 inches long. How many beads will she need?

_____ beads

1 823 ÷ 5 = _____

2
1,000	50	1,050
x 2	x 2	x 2

3 What is the perimeter?

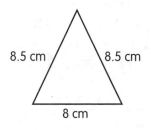

8.5 cm   8.5 cm
8 cm   _____ cm

4 How long is each side of a square that has the same perimeter as the figure in problem 3?

_____ cm

5 Heidi went to the library to check out some books. The books she wanted were on the fifth floor. As she climbed the stairs, she noticed that there were two flights of stairs for each floor, and each flight of stairs had 12 steps. How many steps in all did Heidi climb to reach the fifth floor?

_____ steps

1 Round to the hundreds place to estimate the answer.

1,650 + 436 = _____

2 Solve the problem.

```
  1,650
+   436
-------
```

3 What is the value of **3** in each number?

93,764　_____

306,825　_____

4 List the first ten multiples of 5.

_____ _____ _____ _____ _____

_____ _____ _____ _____ _____

5 Marti climbed a rope attached to the gymnasium ceiling. The ceiling is 20 feet high, and she climbed to within 18 inches of it. How high did Marti climb?

_____ feet

1 $7\overline{)2,016}$

2
```
  111        100        110
x   9      x   9      x   9
-----      -----      -----
```

3 Continue the pattern and write the rule.

100　92　84　76　_____　_____　_____

Rule: _____

4 Which figure is congruent to the white shape in the box?

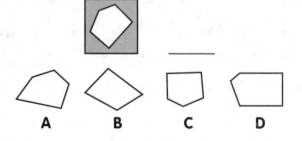

_____

A　　B　　C　　D

5 Laura baby-sat five children for two hours. If she was paid $2.00 per child per hour, how much money did Laura make?

$_____

1. Write the name of the shape to complete each description.

> | hexagon | nonagon | rhombus | trapezoid |

A A _____ has 4 equal sides but no right angles.

B A _____ has 4 sides but only two are parallel.

C A _____ has 9 sides and 9 angles.

D A _____ has 6 sides and 6 angles.

2. How many of each shape above are in the figure below?

A _____   **B** _____   **C** _____   **D** _____

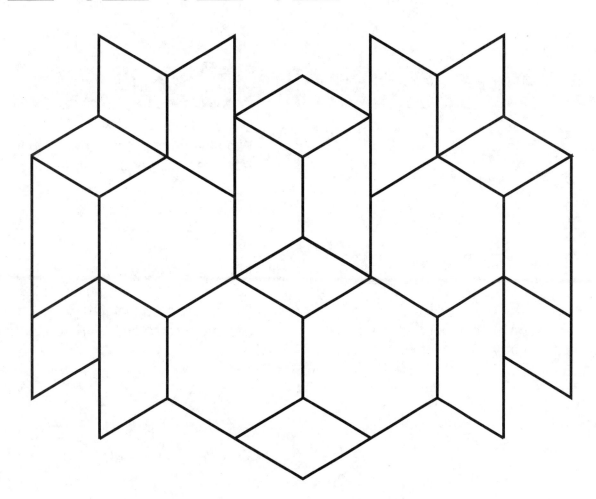

1. Is the equation correct?   **yes   no**
   If **no**, correct any errors.

   $3 \times 23 = 66$

2. Is the equation correct?   **yes   no**
   If **no**, correct any errors.

   $14.3 + 26.4 + 38.2 = 78.9$

3. If the outside temperature was 54 degrees at 2:30 p.m. and 29 degrees at 9:30 p.m., how many degrees did it drop?

   _____ degrees

4. Write $\frac{1}{2}$ as a decimal.   _____

5. Greg gets out of school at 3:20 p.m. His mom picks him up 25 minutes later. At what time does Greg's mom pick him up after school?

   _____

1. $7,200 \div 90 =$ _____

2.
   $$\begin{array}{r} 100 \\ \times\ \ 8 \\ \hline \end{array} \qquad \begin{array}{r} 1,000 \\ \times\ \ \ \ \ 8 \\ \hline \end{array} \qquad \begin{array}{r} 1,010 \\ \times\ \ \ \ \ 8 \\ \hline \end{array}$$

3. Draw an **X** on the number that is least. Circle the number that is greatest.

   $\frac{7}{8}$ 0.25 $1\frac{3}{5}$

4. Write the number twenty-eight thousand fifty-three in standard form.

   _____

5. Anya is watching a football game on TV. She has noticed that every 5 minutes there are 2 commercials. If the game lasts 2 hours, how many commercials will Anya see?

   _____ commercials

1 Estimate the answer.

25 x 11 = _____

2 Solve the problem.

```
   25
 x 11
 ────
```

3 Draw an **X** on the shapes that are congruent.

4 Write the answer to the equation in simplest form.

$5\frac{3}{5} + 7\frac{4}{5} + 6\frac{2}{5} =$ _____

Show your work.

5 At Darian's piano recital, 12 students will each play 2 songs. If each song takes an average of 5 minutes to play, about how long will the recital last?

_____ minutes

1 5)‾1,002‾

2
```
   11          101         1,001
 x  6        x   6        x     6
 ────        ─────        ───────
```

3 Round to the nearest hundred thousand.

389,935 _____

580,234 _____

4 Which is longer?

◯ 1 foot   ◯ 1 meter

5 Lucy has a library book that is 6 days overdue. The library charges 45¢ for the first day and 25¢ each additional day that a book is overdue. How much does Lucy owe the library for her overdue book?

$_____

Nadia, Miguel, and Rashad are taking part in a 12-mile walkathon to help raise money for the homeless shelter in their town. They have collected pledges from friends and neighbors to contribute amounts from 5¢ to 50¢ for each mile they walk in the event. The tally charts below show how many pledges they have collected for each amount.

Nadia	
5¢	卌 I
10¢	III
15¢	卌
25¢	II
30¢	IIII
40¢	II

Miguel	
5¢	卌
20¢	卌 III
25¢	卌
35¢	I
40¢	II
50¢	III

Rashad	
10¢	卌
15¢	IIII
20¢	II
25¢	I
30¢	II
50¢	II

1. Complete a line plot to show the pledges per mile.

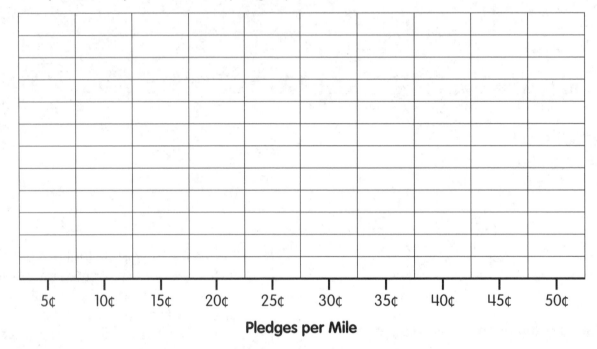

Pledges per Mile

2. If they walk all twelve miles, how much money altogether will
   Nadia, Miguel, and Rashad raise for the homeless shelter? $_____

   Show your work.

1 Is the equation correct? **yes** **no**
If **no**, correct any errors.

$$8,100 \div 9 = 90$$

2 Is the equation correct? **yes** **no**
If **no**, correct any errors.

$$155 - 138 = 117$$

3 List all the factors of 16.

_____

4 What are the coordinates of **X**?

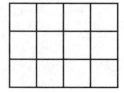

_____

5 Lily wants to make a bouquet of two dozen flowers. She picked 5 roses, 6 daisies, and 7 tulips. How many more flowers does Lily need?

_____ flowers

1 $8)\overline{6,040}$

2 $\begin{array}{r} 4,321 \\ \times \quad 5 \\ \hline \end{array}$

3 What is the area of the rectangle if each block is 1 square centimeter?

_____

4 Which decimal is larger?

○ 0.3   ○ 0.8

5 Jamal's bookcase has five shelves. Each shelf holds fifteen books. If the shelves are two-thirds full, how many books does Jamal have?

_____ books

Show your work.

1 Estimate the answer.

$32 + 39 + 33 + 28 =$ _____

2 Solve the problem.

$$\begin{array}{r} 32 \\ 39 \\ 33 \\ +28 \\ \hline \end{array}$$

3 If $y = 88$, then $y + y =$ _____.

4 Write the correct symbol in the circle.

$$\begin{array}{r} 5{,}220 \\ +13{,}480 \\ \hline \end{array} \bigcirc \begin{array}{r} 13{,}220 \\ + 5{,}480 \\ \hline \end{array}$$

5 Lucy had 24 beanbags and gave $\frac{1}{3}$ of them to her friend Shelley. How many beanbags does Lucy have left?

_____ beanbags

---

1 $245 \div 6 =$ _____

2

$$\begin{array}{r} 1{,}000 \\ \times\quad 8 \\ \hline \end{array} \quad \begin{array}{r} 20 \\ \times 8 \\ \hline \end{array} \quad \begin{array}{r} 7 \\ \times 8 \\ \hline \end{array} \quad \begin{array}{r} 1{,}027 \\ \times\quad 8 \\ \hline \end{array}$$

☐ + ☐ + ☐ = ☐

3 How many lines of symmetry does the figure have? Draw them.

○ 1
○ 2
○ 4

4 Write 0.25 as a fraction. _____

5 Randy and Michelle asked their mother to make pies for the school bake sale. She said that if they could pick enough apples, she had enough flour, sugar, and spices to make 9 apple pies. She needs 4 apples for each pie. How many apples will Randy and Michelle have to pick?

_____ apples

➤ Activity 1

The large cube below contains 27 small cubes. The 4 sides of each small cube alternate light gray and dark gray. The tops and bottoms alternate white and black. Shade what you think the small cube in the very center of the large cube looks like.

 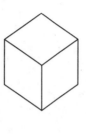

➤ Activity 2

Write the correct symbol in the circle.   **< = >**

1. 450 + 320 ◯ 495 + 265

2. 694 − 452 ◯ 531 − 284

3. 25 x 11 ◯ 35 x 7

4. 80 + 40 + 12 ◯ 90 + 10 + 22

5. 64 ÷ 5 ◯ 88 ÷ 7

6. 912 − 613 ◯ 190 + 50 + 69

7. 30 x 12 ◯ 3,600 ÷ 10

8. $25\frac{1}{4}$ + $34\frac{3}{4}$ ◯ 12 x 7

1   Is the equation correct?   **yes   no**
    If **no**, correct any errors.

    5 x 25 = 120

2   Is the equation correct?   **yes   no**
    If **no**, correct any errors.

    180 ÷ 6 = 300

3   Is 41 a prime or a composite number?

    ○ prime   ○ composite

4   What is the inverse of 240 ÷ 12 = 20?

    _____

5   Cole had 8 pages of math homework last night. If there were 64 problems in all, how many problems were probably on each page?

    _____ problems

1   $4\overline{)804}$

2   $\dfrac{7}{8}$
    $-\dfrac{5}{8}$
    $\overline{}$

3   Round each decimal to the hundredths place.

    206.7239 _____

    494.5088 _____

    99.8902 _____

4   Which fraction is the largest?

    ○ $\dfrac{1}{2}$ ○ $\dfrac{1}{4}$ ○ $\dfrac{1}{3}$

5   Keisha needs postage stamps to mail invitations for her birthday party to 9 friends. If stamps cost 45¢ each, how much will it cost Keisha to mail the invitations?

    $_____

1 Round to the hundreds place to estimate the answer.

3,511 – 946 = _____

2 Solve the problem.

     3,511
   –   946
   ‾‾‾‾‾‾‾

3 I am a number between 10 and 25. I am a multiple of 8, and one of my digits is 2. What number am I?

_____

4 When the net below is folded into a cube, which letter is on the side opposite D?

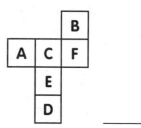

_____

5 Polly collects stickers from the 50 United States. She already has stickers from 34 different states. If she wants at least one sticker from every state, how many more stickers from different states does she need?

_____ states

1 306 ÷ 3 = _____

2   105   1,050
     x   9   x   9
     ‾‾‾‾‾   ‾‾‾‾‾‾‾

3 Write the fraction in simplest form.

⬚⬚⬚⬚⬚⬚⬚⬚⬚⬚ = □/□

4 How many cups are in 3 quarts?

_____ cups

5 When Carmen got up at 7:00 a.m., it was 42 degrees outside. By 2:00 p.m., the temperature had risen 39 degrees. What was the temperature at 2:00 p.m.?

_____ degrees

Each section of the figure below is labeled with a letter. Use the clues to find out what whole number goes in each section and what color each section should be. Complete the chart next to the clues to show your answers.

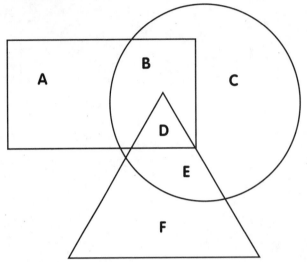

Clues

- The sum of the sections in the triangle is 15.
- The section that is in all three shapes is colored green.
- The rectangle has the red, white, and green sections in it.
- The orange section is the number 8.
- The product of the D section and the blue section is 21.
- The purple section is the number 5.
- Section A is red.
- The sum of the sections in the rectangle is 11.
- Section E is blue.
- The sum of the sections in the circle is 20.
- The sum of sections A and B is 8.

	Number	Color
A		
B		
C		
D		
E		
F		

1 Is the equation correct?   **yes   no**
If **no**, correct any errors.

$50 \times 40 = 200$

2 Is the equation correct?   **yes   no**
If **no**, correct any errors.

$157.4 - 92.9 = 64.5$

3 What place does **8** have in the number 15.8?

○ ones
○ tens
○ tenths

4 Write the correct symbol in the circle.

<   =   >

73 ◯ 7.4

5 Brandon is collecting shells on the beach.
If he finds a shell after every three steps
he takes, how many shells will he find
after taking 189 steps?

_____ shells

Show your work.

1 $510 \div 3 =$ _____

2   141
      x   7

3 Name the radius.

_____

Name the diameter.

_____

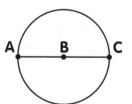

4 How many rectangles are there?

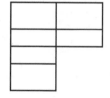

_____ rectangles

5 Bella is swinging across the monkey bars.
There are 16 bars from one end to the
other. If Bella starts at the first bar and
skips two bars each time she swings,
how many bars will she touch in all?

_____ bars

1 Estimate the answer.

285 + 429 + 802 = _____

2 Solve the problem.

```
  285
  429
+ 802
```

3 Draw an **X** on the number line to show **13**.

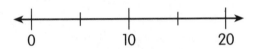

```
0        10        20
```

4 15 dimes + 7 nickels = $_____

5 Seth is pulling weeds in his backyard. His dad will pay him 5¢ for each weed he pulls. If Seth pulls 208 weeds, how much will his dad pay him?

$_____

1 11)‾2,000

2
```
  106          106
x   8        x  10
```

3 How do you know if a number is divisible by 5?

_____

_____

_____

4 A soup recipe calls for $1\frac{1}{4}$ pounds of pinto beans. A package of beans contains 28 ounces. Are there enough beans in one package to make the soup?

○ **yes**   ○ **no**

5 An 8-ounce can of soup costs 88¢. A 24-ounce can of soup costs $2.40. Which size can is the better buy?

○ 8-ounce can   ○ 24-ounce can

Daily Math Practice • EMC 6714 • © Evan-Moor Corp.

Favorite Books	Boys	Girls
Beezus and Ramona	2	4
Diary of a Wimpy Kid	4	4
The Snow Goose	3	6
James and the Giant Peach	5	4
The Earth Dragon Awakes	7	2
Jumanji	5	3

Make a graph to show the information in the table above. Remember to include a title, scales, axis labels, and a key.

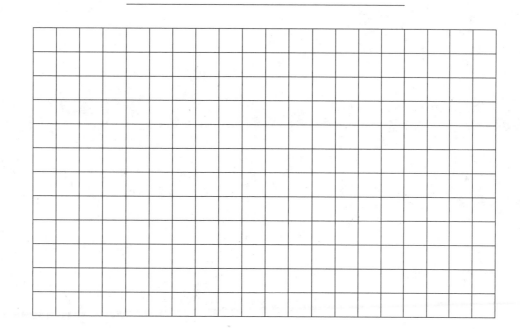

1 Is the equation correct? **yes no**
If **no**, correct any errors.

79.3 + 12.7 = 82.1

2 Is the equation correct? **yes no**
If **no**, correct any errors.

900 ÷ 90 = 100

3 Mark the cube that comes next in the pattern.

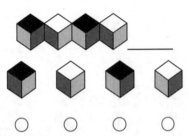

○   ○   ○   ○

4 Write the numbers in order from smallest to largest.

0.9 $\frac{3}{4}$ 0.5 $\frac{1}{3}$ $1\frac{1}{4}$

_____ _____ _____ _____ _____

5 Bruce is a very fast reader. He can read about 40 pages in an hour. About how long will it take him to read a 140-page book?

_____ hours

1 3 × 327 = _____

2 2)‾6‾6‾3‾

3 Write each answer in simplest form.

$8\frac{1}{9} + 4\frac{2}{9} =$ _____ $\frac{1}{10} × 5 =$ _____

$6\frac{3}{4} + 1\frac{1}{4} =$ _____ $\frac{3}{4} × 2 =$ _____

4 Write the number six hundred two in expanded form.

_____

5 On her spelling test, Julia guessed on 10 of the 100 words. If half of the words that she guessed on are correct, and all the words that she didn't guess on are correct, how many words will she have wrong on the whole test?

_____ words

1 Estimate the answer.

$38 + 47 - 71 =$ _____

2 Solve the problem.

$38 + 47 - 71 =$ _____

3 How many?

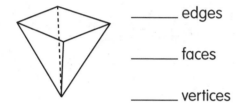

_____ edges

_____ faces

_____ vertices

4 Write all the multiples of 9 that are more than 20 and less than 100.

_____

5 Alan and Jeff washed cars together all day to earn money for summer camp. They charged $10.00 per car and agreed to split all the money equally at the end of the day. Alan washed 12 cars, and Jeff washed 9 cars. How much money did each boy get at the end of the day?

$_____

1 $3,001 \div 300 =$ _____

2
$$
\begin{array}{r} 1,041 \\ \times \quad 5 \\ \hline \end{array}
\qquad
\begin{array}{r} 1,041 \\ \times \quad 10 \\ \hline \end{array}
$$

3 Find the perimeter and the area.

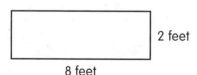

2 feet

8 feet

perimeter _____

area _____

4 How many feet are in 3 yards?

_____ feet

5 Ming had a box of chalk in her backpack. While walking home from school, she decided to draw a chalk line on the sidewalk all the way to her house. The first piece of chalk lasted for two-thirds of a block. If she had 11 more pieces of chalk in the box, for how many blocks in all was she able to draw a line?

_____ blocks

The clock in the center shows the time Ben's birthday party ended. Ben opened his presents 45 minutes earlier. The kids were all eating cake 25 minutes before that, and they were playing games 30 minutes before eating cake. The party started 20 minutes before the games began.

Draw hands on each clock and write the time under it to show when the party started and when each activity took place.

Party Started

_____

Played Games

_____

Party Ended

Ate Cake

_____

Opened Presents

_____

1 Is the equation correct?   **yes**   **no**
If **no**, correct any errors.

2 x 345 = 708

2 Is the equation correct?   **yes**   **no**
If **no**, correct any errors.

206.4 – 103.8 = 102.6

3 Henry has $6.28. What is the largest
number of each coin he could have?

quarters _____

dimes _____

4 Write the fraction $\frac{79}{100}$ in decimal form.

_____

5 Diana and Becky were on the same
soccer team and took turns being the
goalie. They stopped 9 out of every
10 shots made against them. If the
other team scored 3 points, how many
balls did Diana and Becky stop from
going into the net?

_____ balls

1 285 ÷ 5 = _____

2   2,162
     x   4
   _____

3 Complete each equation below if $m = 75$.

$m \times 3 =$ _____

$m \div 3 =$ _____

4 Round 6.48 to the nearest whole number.

_____

5 Dylan and Kendra were cleaning the
garage and found 6 boxes filled with
hats. If there were 15 hats in each box,
how many hats did Dylan and Kendra
find altogether?

_____ hats

1 Estimate the answer.

69 x 21 = _____

2 Solve the problem.

69
x 21

3 How many cubic units are in the figure?

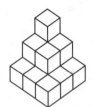

_____ cubic units

4 Write the fraction for 0.08 in simplest form.

_____

5 Kyle played video games for 3 hours and 45 minutes on Friday night. If he started at 5:50 p.m. and played straight through, at what time did he stop playing?

_____

1 8)568

2 1,041
x   8

3 List all the factors of 100.

_____

4 Which figure is congruent to the shaded one?

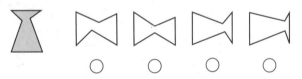

○   ○   ○   ○

5 Jamal's band learns lots of new songs. The band learns a new song every four days. At this rate, how many new songs will the band learn in four weeks?

_____ songs

Look at the graph to answer the questions.

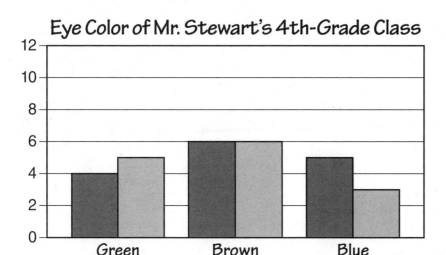

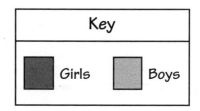

1. How many students in all are in Mr. Stewart's class? _____

2. How many students in all have brown eyes? _____

3. How many boys have blue eyes? _____

4. How many more girls have blue eyes than green eyes? _____

5. What fraction of all students with green eyes are boys? _____

6. What fraction of all girls have brown eyes?
   Write the fraction as a decimal. _____

7. What fraction of all students in Mr. Stewart's class have blue eyes? _____

8. What is the ratio of boys with blue eyes to boys with brown eyes? _____

1 Is the equation correct?   **yes   no**
If **no**, correct any errors.

$648 \div 8 = 81$

2 Is the equation correct?   **yes   no**
If **no**, correct any errors.

$47.4 - 29.5 = 17.1$

3 Which fraction is larger?

○ $\frac{3}{4}$

○ $\frac{2}{3}$

4 Estimate 11 x 299. _____

5 Travis was walking to school when he saw some friends walking a block ahead of him. After running to catch up with his friends, his heart was beating 24 beats every 10 seconds. At this rate, how many times would his heart beat in 3 minutes?

_____ times

Show your work.

1 $4\overline{)7,612}$

2 $\frac{3}{4}$ $\frac{3}{4}$
     $-\frac{2}{4}$ $+\frac{2}{4}$
    _____   _____

3 Draw the rest of the figure if the bold line is a line of symmetry.

4 How many quarts are in 4 gallons?

_____ quarts

5 Jenny is writing a book. She has written 47 pages so far. If she wants the book to be 90 pages long, how many more pages does she have to write?

_____ pages

1 Estimate the answer.

$\frac{4}{5} \times 3 =$ _____

2 Solve the problem. Write the answer in simplest form.

$\frac{4}{5}$

$\times\ 3$

_____

3 The temperature at 5:00 p.m. was 45 degrees. Four hours later, it had fallen 16 degrees. What was the temperature at 9:00 p.m.?

_____ degrees

4 Find the area.

3 m

13 m

_____

5 Emily was born on March 2, 1999. If her brother Evan is three years and three months younger than she is, in what month and year was he born?

_____

1 960 ÷ 8 = _____

2 1,510
  $\times$ 5

3 Match the angles with their names.

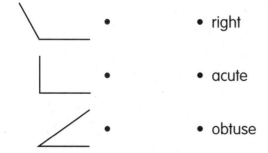

•   • right

•   • acute

•   • obtuse

4 Write five thousand seven hundred eight and eight hundredths in expanded form.

_____

5 In how many different ways can Leo, Jessie, and Franchesca line up to buy their tickets at the movies?

_____ different ways

Show your work.

Write the fractions or mixed numbers for the shaded parts. Then solve the equations.
Write the answers in simplest form.

1. 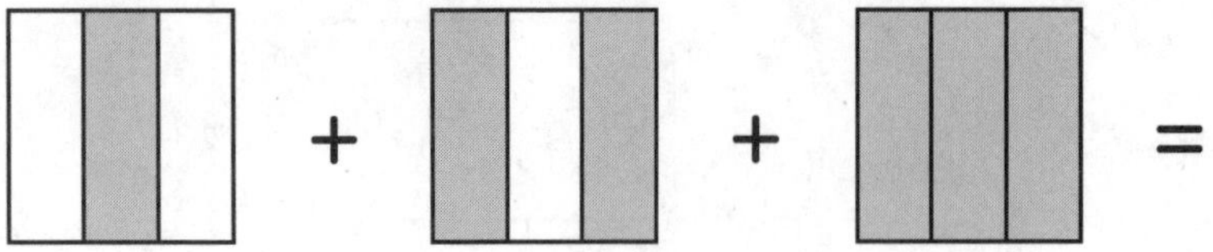 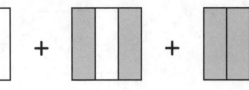 = _____

_____   _____   _____

2. = _____

_____   _____

3. 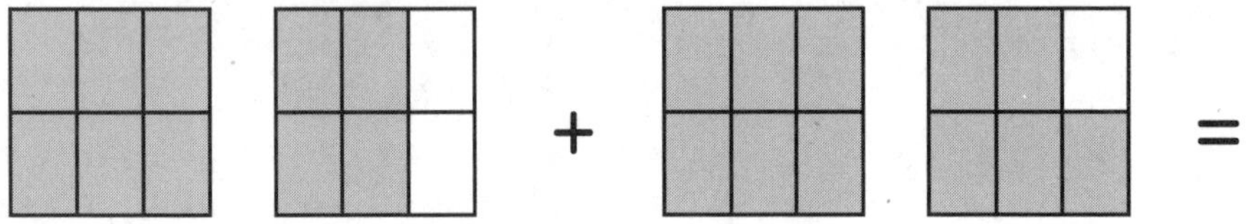 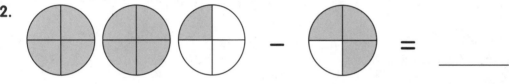 = _____

_____   _____

4. 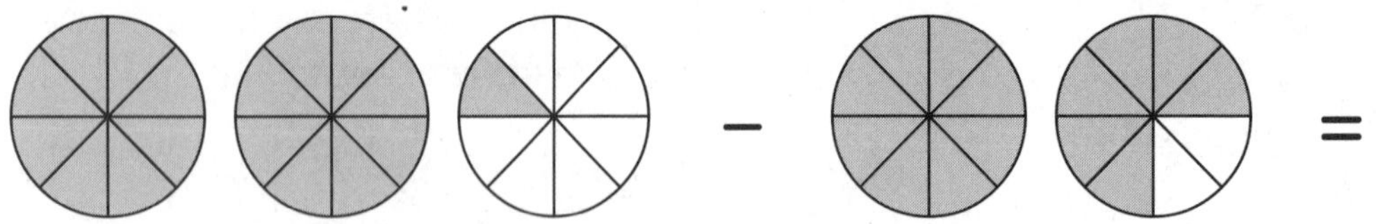 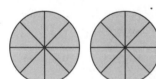 = _____

_____   _____

1 Is the equation correct?   **yes**   **no**
   If **no**, correct any errors.

   3,507 – 753 = 3,254

2 Is the equation correct?   **yes**   **no**
   If **no**, correct any errors.

   214 + 359 + 106 = 699

3 What number can you add to any other
   number and always get that same
   number as the answer?

   _____

4 Continue the pattern.

   80 70 60 _____ _____ _____

5 Justin and Olive were racing around the
   school's track. Olive finished in 1 minute and
   18 seconds. Justin finished in 75 seconds.
   Who was faster?

   ◯ Justin   ◯ Olive

   Explain.

   _____

   _____

---

1 6)‾6‾0‾6‾

2   104
     x   9

3 Draw an **X** on the grid to show the
   coordinates (13, 8).

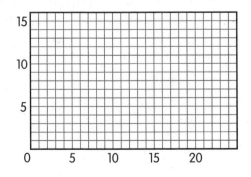

4 Write the numbers in order from greatest
   to least.

   0.59 $\frac{11}{12}$ $1\frac{1}{8}$ $\frac{2}{3}$

   _____ _____ _____ _____

5 Nate and Chris were walking along the
   river, throwing stones into the water. Every
   three steps, they would each throw one
   stone. If they each walked ninety steps,
   how many stones would they throw into
   the river altogether?

   _____ stones

1   Round to the nearest hundred thousand to estimate the answer.

7,168,259 – 805,317 = _____

2   Solve the problem.

    7,168,259
–   805,317
_____

3   What flat shape has four sides that are all the same length but has no right angles?

_____

4   On a standard six-sided die, the sum of the numbers on opposite sides of the cube always equal 7. Fill in the missing dots on each die below.

5   Mike is twice as old as his younger brother Matt. If Mike is 12, how old is Matt?

_____ years old

1   427 ÷ 7 = _____

2   1,051
   x   7
_____

3   Name the pairs of parallel lines.

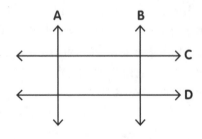

_____

4   Victor drew an equilateral triangle. He made the base 4 centimeters long. How long were each of the other two sides?

_____ cm

5   Cheryl gives her dogs a bath in a big metal tub. She fills the tub with 20 gallons of water to begin with. Then she uses another 28 gallons of water to rinse the dogs and 9 gallons of water to clean out the tub. How much water does Cheryl use altogether?

_____ gallons

If you put **6** into this function machine, **24** comes out.

If you put **8** into this function machine, **28** comes out.

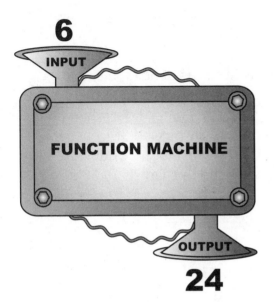

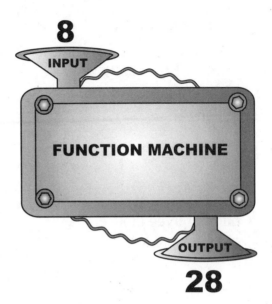

1. Figure out a rule that works for **both** machines. **Rule:** _____

Show your work.

2. Use the rule to complete the function tables below.

Input	Output
6	24
2	
9	
12	
4	
10	

Input	Output
8	28
5	
11	
3	
0	
7	

1. Is the equation correct?   **yes**   **no**
If **no**, correct any errors.

   $9,053 - 6,845 = 3,208$

2. Is the equation correct?   **yes**   **no**
If **no**, correct any errors.

   $201.6 + 725.4 = 927.0$

3. Write the number three thousand sixty-eight in standard form.

   _____

4. List the first four multiples of 12.

   _____   _____   _____   _____

5. Trent's watch runs at half the speed it should. In other words, the hands on the watch move only a half hour when an hour of time has really passed. If Trent sets his watch correctly at 8 a.m., what time will it show when the real time is 10:30 a.m.?

   _____

1. $763 \div 7 =$ _____

2. $\begin{array}{r} 256 \\ \times\ \ \ 5 \\ \hline \end{array}$ $\begin{array}{r} 256 \\ \times\ 10 \\ \hline \end{array}$

3. What are the next two figures in the pattern?

    _____ _____

4. What three-dimensional shape is a basketball?

   _____

5. Jeremy and five of his friends want to go whale watching. Tickets cost $38.00 each. How much will it cost Jeremy and his friends altogether?

   $_____

1 Estimate the answer.

$152 + (31 \times 9) =$ _____

2 Solve the problem.

$152 + (31 \times 9) =$ _____

3 Which weighs more?

○ 1 gram   ○ 1 pound

4 The graph below shows how Marta spent the $40.00 she earned baby-sitting. Approximately how much money did she spend on food?

■ Food
□ Recreation
▦ Books/Videos
■ CDs/Music

$ _____

5 Alex got a new skateboard for his birthday. He left the house at 4:55 p.m. Ten minutes later, he crashed into his friend's bike. What time was it when Alex hit the bike?

_____

1 $3\overline{)2{,}136}$

2
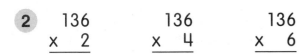

136	136	136
× 2	× 4	× 6

3 Find the perimeter.

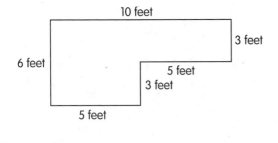

10 feet
3 feet
6 feet
5 feet
3 feet
5 feet

_____

4 What is the area of the figure in problem 3?

_____

5 Jin and Chen are painting a fence. Each plank on the fence takes one person about 3 minutes to paint. If there are 8 sections of fence with 12 planks in each section, about how many hours will it take Jin and Chen to do the job?

_____

➤ Activity 1

Use the clues to determine the order of six school bus stops. The first stop should be at the house that is closest to the school. The last stop should be at the house that is farthest from the school.

Clues

- Ginny's house is farther from the school than Henry's, but not as far as Lou's.
- Henry's house is closer to the school than Dan's.
- Karla's house is closer to the school than both Vicki's and Dan's but is farther than Ginny's.
- Vicki's house is the last stop.
- Lou's stop is immediately after Karla's.

1. _____   4. _____

2. _____   5. _____

3. _____   6. _____

➤ Activity 2

Name the shape of the base on each solid figure.

1.

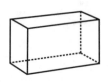

_____

3.

_____

2.

_____

4.

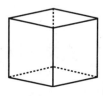

_____

1 Is the equation correct? **yes** **no**
   If **no**, correct any errors.

   3 x 298 = 874

2 Is the equation correct? **yes** **no**
   If **no**, correct any errors.

   17.5 – 6.8 = 0.7

3 Round to the greatest place.

   38.97   _____

   7.45   _____

   10.009 _____

4 Draw the radius of circle 1.
   Draw the diameter of circle 2.

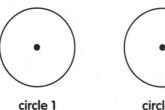

   circle 1   circle 2

5 Marcus is playing dodge ball with his
   friends. He catches 2 out of every 5 balls
   thrown in his direction. If he catches
   14 balls, how many balls were thrown
   at him?

   _____ balls

1 4,806 ÷ 6 = _____

2 $\begin{array}{r} 2,507 \\ \times \quad 6 \\ \hline \end{array}$

3 List the next four multiples of each number
   and circle the common multiples.

   __6__ _____ _____ _____ _____

   __8__ _____ _____ _____ _____

4 What are the common factors of 6 and 8?

   _____

5 Emma baby-sits for $4.50 an hour. Her
   sister Sara helps her sometimes, and
   they share the money. Last Saturday, Sara
   helped Emma baby-sit for 8 hours. If they
   split the money evenly, how much did
   each girl earn?

   $_____

1 $(8 + 7) \times 8 = $ _____

2 Solve for y.

$y + 4 = 25$ $\qquad$ $y = $ _____

3 Draw the rest of the figure if the bold line represents a line of symmetry.

4 How many inches are in 4 yards?

_____ inches

5 Dominic mows lawns on Saturdays to earn money. He is paid $5.00 for each lawn he mows. If he mows 4 lawns every Saturday, how much will he earn in 6 weeks?

$_____

---

1 $10\overline{)700}$ $\qquad$ $10\overline{)800}$ $\qquad$ $10\overline{)900}$

2
$\begin{array}{r} 1,110 \\ \times \quad 7 \\ \hline \end{array}$ $\qquad$ $\begin{array}{r} 1,110 \\ \times \quad 8 \\ \hline \end{array}$ $\qquad$ $\begin{array}{r} 1,110 \\ \times \quad 9 \\ \hline \end{array}$

3 Name the pairs of perpendicular lines.

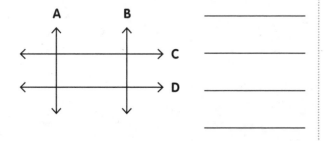

_____

_____

_____

_____

4 Write the correct symbol in the circle.

< $\quad$ = $\quad$ >

$\frac{1}{3}$ ◯ 0.25

$\frac{2}{5}$ ◯ 0.40

5 Yasmin needs new shelves for her books. She has about 200 books. If she can fit about 30 books on each shelf, how many shelves does she need?

_____ shelves

➤ Activity 1

Use the digits **3**, **6**, **8**, and **9** to answer the questions. Use each digit only once in a number.

1. What is the smallest, even four-digit number you can make?   _____

2. What is the largest, odd four-digit number you can make?   _____

3. List all the four-digit numbers you can make that are the multiples of 5.

   _____

4. Write two four-digit numbers that are the multiples of 4.

   _____

➤ Activity 2

Draw an **X** to show the place of each digit **5**.

	millions	hundred thousands	ten thousands	thousands	hundreds	tens	ones	tenths	hundredths
635,751									
56,944									
805.26									
7,534,502									
53.75									
412,500.05									
5,123,855									
5.56									
358,235									
125,673.55									

1 Is the equation correct? **yes** **no**
If **no**, correct any errors.

$3,228 \div 4 = 807$

2 Is the equation correct? **yes** **no**
If **no**, correct any errors.

$125 + 63 + 8 = 296$

3 Write the correct symbol in the circle.

< = >

1 gallon ◯ 1 liter

10 ounces ◯ 1 pint

15 centiliters ◯ $1\frac{1}{2}$ deciliters

4 A roll of nickels is worth $2.00. How many nickels are in four rolls?

_____ nickels

5 As Jan was washing glasses and putting them away, she noticed that she could stack 4 glasses on top of each other on the cupboard shelf. If she has 23 glasses to put away, how many full stacks of glasses can she make?

_____ stacks

1 $5\overline{)225}$ $5\overline{)255}$ $5\overline{)552}$

2   776
    × 4

3 Write the correct symbol in the circle.

< = >

17 ◯ 2.95

1.7 ◯ 2.95

4 Round the difference of 198 − 49 to the nearest ten.

_____

5 Gary needs to buy nails to build a house for his dog. He needs 20 nails for the roof and 18 nails for the floor. The front and back sides each need 15 nails, and the other two sides each need 12 nails. How many nails altogether does Gary need to buy?

_____ nails

1 $4 - (3 \div 3) =$ _____

2 Solve for *x*.

$x - 72 = 28$ $x =$ _____

3 Which two figures are congruent?

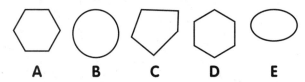

  A   **B**   **C**   **D**   **E**

_____ and _____

4 Each section on the number line is one unit. Label each mark.

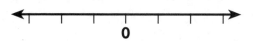

5 Luke's dad said that he would pay Luke $4.00 each to wash the family's two cars. Then Luke's neighbor said that he would pay Luke $5.00 to wash his car. If Luke washes all three cars, how much money will he make?

$_____

1 $3,024 \div 3 =$ _____

2   12
     x 43
     ‾‾‾‾

3 How many cubes are in the rectangular prism?

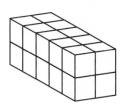

_____ cubes

4 Draw an **X** on the number line to show **68**.

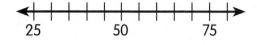

5 On her way to school, Tina noticed that 1 of every 3 houses she walks by has a dog in the backyard. If she walks past 18 houses, how many dogs will she see?

_____ dogs

Levi's Scout troop was trying to decide what kinds of toppings to have on the pizzas they planned to sell to raise money for camping gear. The Scouts asked their family members which toppings they preferred. The table to the right shows the responses. Use the information in the table to complete the line plot below.

Pizza Toppings	Number of People
pepperoni	15
sausage	9
mushrooms	12
black olives	5
onions	3
anchovies	1

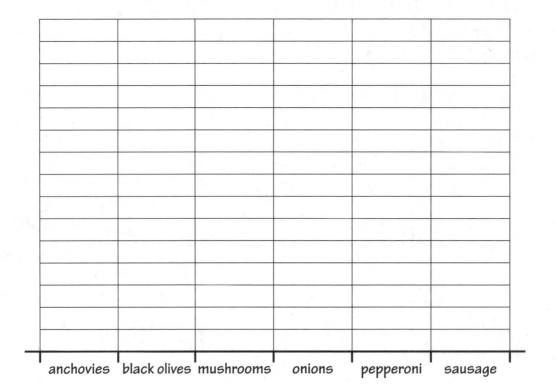

Look at the line plot to help you answer the following question.

Based on the information they gathered, the Scouts have decided to sell two kinds of pizzas. Each kind will have a meat topping and one additional topping. Which additional topping should they combine with each meat topping below to have two kinds of pizza that will probably sell equally well?

1. pepperoni and _____

2. sausage and _____

Daily Math Practice • EMC 6714 • © Evan-Moor Corp.

1 Is the equation correct?   **yes**   **no**
If **no**, correct any errors.

823.6 + 147.5 = 970.1

2 Is the equation correct?   **yes**   **no**
If **no**, correct any errors.

954 − 396 = 558

3 How many lines of symmetry does the figure have?

○ 1
○ 2
○ 4

4 Which is smaller?

○ $\frac{1}{3}$ ○ $\frac{3}{4}$

5 Liam and Terry are baking cookies for a party. Including themselves, there will be 15 people at the party, and they want to have at least 3 cookies for each person. How many dozen cookies do Liam and Terry need to bake?

○ 3 dozen   ○ 4 dozen   ○ 5 dozen

---

1 1,604 ÷ 4 = _____

2
$$\begin{array}{ccc} 231 & 231 & 231 \\ \times\ 10 & \times\ 11 & \times\ 12 \end{array}$$

3 Use four different prime numbers to complete the two equations below.

_____ + _____ = 30

30 − _____ = _____

4 If the temperature of 8 degrees dropped 10 degrees, what would the new temperature be?

_____ degrees

5 Toshi watched TV on Friday night for three and a half hours straight. If he started at 8:45 p.m., at what time did he stop?

_____

1. $(20 - 10) - 8 = $ _____

   $20 - (10 - 8) = $ _____

2. Solve for y.

   $16 + y = 37$ $y = $ _____

3. Use $n = 5$ to complete the equations.

   $253 + n - 8 = $ _____

   $2 - \frac{1}{n} = $ _____

   $n \times 12 = $ _____

4. What is the sixth letter of the alphabet?

   _____

5. Derek and Joel were playing catch with a water balloon. They started out standing right next to each other. Then every time one boy threw and the other boy successfully caught the balloon, they both stepped backward one foot. They continued this pattern until one of them dropped the balloon, which happened on the thirteenth throw. How far apart were the boys by then?

   _____ feet

1. $9\overline{)4,509}$

2. $\begin{array}{r} \frac{7}{9} \\ -\frac{5}{9} \\ \hline \end{array}$ $\begin{array}{r} \frac{8}{9} \\ -\frac{5}{9} \\ \hline \end{array}$ $\begin{array}{r} 1 \\ -\frac{5}{9} \\ \hline \end{array}$

3. Write each fraction in simplest form.

   $\frac{3}{6} = $ _____ $\frac{2}{10} = $ _____

   $\frac{4}{12} = $ _____ $\frac{6}{8} = $ _____

4. Write the number for seven million eight hundred ten thousand twenty-two.

   _____

5. Hannah is half as old as her sister Beth, who is half as old as their brother Rick. If Rick is 16, how old is Hannah?

   _____ years old

Find the perimeter and the area of each figure.

1.

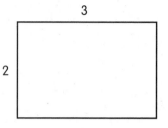

_____ units

_____ square units

Show your work.

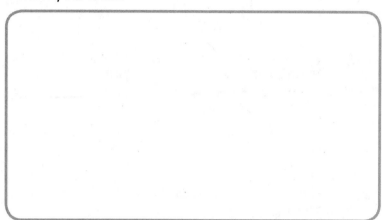

2.

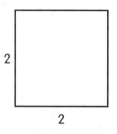

_____ units

_____ square units

Show your work.

3.

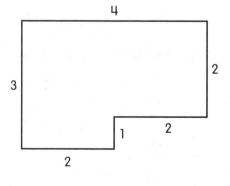

_____ units

_____ square units

Show your work.

1 Is the equation correct?   **yes**   **no**
If **no**, correct any errors.

$724 \times 6 = 4{,}444$

2 Is the equation correct?   **yes**   **no**
If **no**, correct any errors.

$(8.69 - 1.26) + 2.57 = 10$

3 Write the number two hundred thousand nine hundred.

_____

4 What number times any number you pick always equals the same number as the answer?

_____

5 Zack put a clicker on his bicycle wheel so that every time it hits the top of the wheel, it clicks. If each click means that Zack has gone one and a half meters, how far has he gone after twelve clicks?

_____ meters

1 $4{,}024 \div 8 =$ _____

2
$$\begin{array}{r} 101 \\ \times\ 10 \\ \hline \end{array} \qquad \begin{array}{r} 101 \\ \times\ 15 \\ \hline \end{array} \qquad \begin{array}{r} 101 \\ \times\ 20 \\ \hline \end{array}$$

3 What is the smallest number that is greater than the largest number listed below and has all the numbers in the list as factors?

1, 2, 3, 4, 6, 8, 12   _____

4 Which fraction equals $1\frac{3}{8}$?

◯ $\frac{10}{8}$ ◯ $\frac{11}{8}$ ◯ $\frac{12}{8}$

5 Sharise was coloring a design with her new box of 64 crayons. There were so many spaces in the design that she had to use each crayon 3 times. How many spaces were there?

_____ spaces

1 (350 − 125) + (150 − 25) = _____

2 Solve for y.

210 + y = 840   y = _____

3 List the multiples of 3 and 4 that are less than 25.

3 _____

4 _____

4 Using the information from problem 3, what is the smallest common multiple of 3 and 4?

_____

5 Juanita has four coins that total 50¢. What are the four coins?

_____

_____

1 $9\overline{)729}$

2   16
    × 62
  _____

3 Which shape has four sides with only one pair of opposite sides that are parallel?

○ parallelogram
○ rhombus
○ trapezoid

4 What are the next two numbers in the pattern?

5   13   29   61   _____   _____

5 Casey is thinking of a number. Use the clues below to guess the number.

- It is a three-digit number.
- The ones digit is less than 8.
- The tens digit is 2 less than the ones digit.
- The hundreds digit is 3 less than the tens digit.
- The number is odd.

_____

Pete earns $10.00 a week by doing household chores. He spends some of the money and saves the rest. Last year, Pete kept track of how much money he spent each month.

Month	Earned	Spent
January	$40.00	$25.00
February	$40.00	$15.00
March	$50.00	$25.00
April	$40.00	$15.00
May	$50.00	$20.00
June	$40.00	$60.00

Month	Earned	Spent
July	$40.00	$25.00
August	$50.00	$35.00
September	$40.00	$30.00
October	$40.00	$20.00
November	$40.00	$10.00
December	$50.00	$70.00

Make a line graph on the grid to show Pete's savings account **total** at the end of each month.

Pete's Savings

1 Is the equation correct?   **yes   no**
If **no**, correct any errors.

$3{,}500 \div 10 = 350$

2 Is the equation correct?   **yes   no**
If **no**, correct any errors.

$45.3 + 17.3 = 52.6$

3 Round to the nearest tenth.

14.82 _____

21.66 _____

8.51 _____

4 Continue the pattern.

△ ☆ △ ☆ ☆ △ ☆ ☆ ☆

_____ _____ _____ _____ _____

5 Nolan is the pitcher on his baseball team. He throws a curve ball that only one-third of the batters can hit. If forty-five players attempt to hit Nolan's curve ball, how many actually hit it?

_____ players

1 $2\overline{)8{,}410}$ $4\overline{)8{,}410}$

2 $\begin{array}{r} 27 \\ \times\,76 \\ \hline \end{array}$

3 Erika has twice as many plus 5 more colored pencils than her friend Jana. If Jana has 13 colored pencils, how many does Erika have?

_____ colored pencils

4 What does 10 tenths equal?

○ 10.0   ○ 1.0   ○ 0.10

5 What is the ordered pair for **X**?

_____

1 (80 + 29) − (79 + 3) = _____

2 Solve for *x*.

$520 \div x = 52$ *x* = _____

3 Complete the table.

Feet	Inches
1	12
____	24
3	____
____	____
____	____

4 Round 2,097.815 to the hundreds place.

_____

5 Suzanne wants to buy a ring that costs $27.00. She has $6.50 in her wallet, she will get her $12.00 allowance tomorrow, and her sister owes her $4.75. How much more money does Suzanne need?

$_____

1 1,596 ÷ 3 = _____

2   38
     × 57
   ------

3 Mark every statement that is true about the angle.

○ It is an obtuse angle.
○ It is an acute angle.
○ It measures less than 90°.
○ It measures more than 90°.

4 What shape is the base of a cylinder?

_____

5 Skip counted his change. It totaled $6.73. He had 18 pennies, 14 quarters, 2 half dollars, and 5 dimes. How many nickels did he have?

_____ nickels

Max, Angela, Leann, and Mitch were getting ready to go on their family vacations. They were all leaving from San Diego, California. Use the following clues to help you figure out the last name of each child, that family's vacation destination, and their mode of transportation.

Clues

- The Medina family went to Hawaii by either plane or ship.
- Angela's family traveled by car to Wyoming.
- Max's family went by train.
- The Tseu family went to Florida.
- The Carlson family did not go to New York, but another family did.
- The Rodriguez boy got sick on the train ride to his family's destination.
- The Tseu family's daughter is an only child.
- The family traveling by plane went to Florida.

	Last Name	Destination	Transportation
Max			
Angela			
Leann			
Mitch			

1   Is the equation correct?   **yes**   **no**
If **no**, correct any errors.

$58.43 + 81.26 = 39.69$

2   Is the equation correct?   **yes**   **no**
If **no**, correct any errors.

$33 \times 23 = 759$

3   Estimate the products.

$99 \times 41 =$ _____

$56 \times 13 =$ _____

4   List all the factors of 18.

_____

5   Marlene is typing a report that has about 300 words in it. If it takes her one minute to type 25 words, about how long will it take her to type the report?

_____ minutes

---

1 $2{,}412 \div 4 =$ _____

2
$$\begin{array}{r} 75 \\ \times\,41 \\ \hline \end{array}$$

3   Is 49 a prime or a composite number? Explain your answer.

_____

_____

_____

4   If $p = 5$, then $p \times 18 =$ _____.

5   Charlie feeds grasshoppers to his pet snake. It takes Charlie about 2 minutes to catch each grasshopper. If he needs 13 grasshoppers, how long will it take him to catch all of them?

_____ minutes

1 16 − (4 + 1) = _____

   (16 − 4) + 1 = _____

2 Solve for x.

   $x \div 4 = 30$ $x =$ _____

3 At Jesse's party, 10 people wanted lemon-lime soda and 13 people wanted cola. What was the ratio of people wanting lemon-lime to the people wanting cola?

   ○ 13:10   ○ 10:13   ○ 1:3

4 Does this figure have at least one line of symmetry?

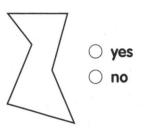

   ○ **yes**
   ○ **no**

5 Chase rode a Ferris wheel 93 times around, one lap after the other. If each lap of the Ferris wheel took 20 seconds, how long was Chase's ride?

   _____ minutes

1 6)1,836

2   52
   ×87

3 Solve the problem. Show your answer in simplest form.

   $\frac{1}{8} \times 10 =$ _____

4 Which is heavier?

   ○ 1 ton   ○ 1 kg

5 Rachel and her sister each have saved $12.75 to buy a present for their mother. If the present costs $25.45, do they have enough money?

   ○ **yes**   ○ **no**

Use the map to answer the questions.

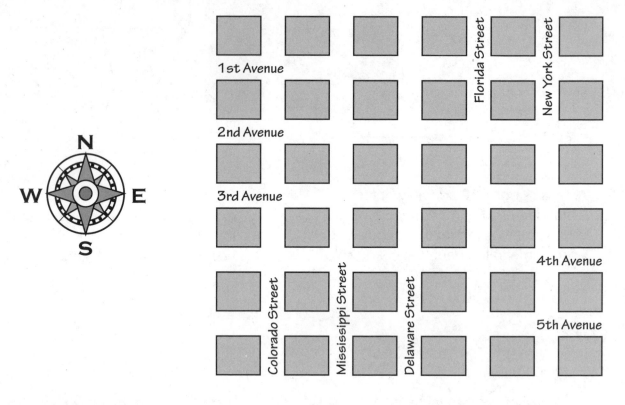

1. Dawn starts at the intersection of Delaware Street and 3rd Avenue. She walks 2 blocks north, 1 block east, 4 blocks south, and turns right. She goes 2 more blocks and turns right before going another 1 block. Where does Dawn end up?

   _____

2. Duke starts at the intersection of New York Street and 2nd Avenue. He walks 4 blocks west and 3 blocks south. Then he turns left and walks 3 more blocks. Where is Duke and in which direction is he heading?

   _____

3. If Duke wants to walk back to where he started, which **two** of the following directions will get him there?

   ○ Go 3 blocks north, turn left, and go another 1 block.

   ○ Go 1 block east and 3 blocks north.

   ○ Go straight 1 block, turn left, and go straight 3 blocks.

1 Is the equation correct?   **yes   no**
   If **no**, correct any errors.

   $\frac{3}{5} + \frac{1}{5} = \frac{2}{5}$

2 Is the equation correct?   **yes   no**
   If **no**, correct any errors.

   $980 + 120 = 1{,}110$

3 How many?

   _____ feet = 1 mile

   _____ meters = 1 kilometer

4 What is the area of the rectangle?

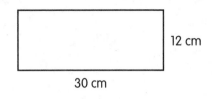

   12 cm

   30 cm

   _____

5 Each of Bryan's six dogs eats $2\frac{1}{2}$ cups
   of dog food every day. If a 20-pound
   bag of dog food contains approximately
   50 cups, how many days can Bryan feed
   all his dogs with one bag?

   _____ days

---

1 $328 \div 8 =$ _____

2 $\begin{array}{r} 319 \\ \times\ 28 \\ \hline \end{array}$

3 Which is larger?

   $\frac{1}{2}$ or $\frac{2}{3}$ _____

   $\frac{6}{8}$ or $\frac{5}{6}$ _____

4 What place value does the **5** have in
   598.3?

   _____

5 Dominque was putting her CDs into her
   new CD racks. If each rack holds 24 CDs,
   how many CDs will 8 racks hold?

   _____ CDs

1 $(7 \times 8) \div 2 = $ _____

2 Solve for x.

$450 \div x = 3$ $x = $ _____

3 Which two figures are congruent?

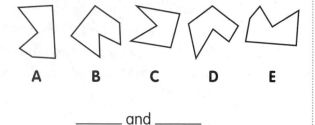

A   **B**   **C**   **D**   **E**

_____ and _____

4 Using the digits **1**, **2**, and **3** only once in each number, show all the different three-digit numbers you can make.

_____

_____

5 Dee likes listening to the radio. The radio station plays a different song about every three minutes. If Dee hears 25 songs, about how long has she been listening?

_____ minutes

1 $7\overline{)4,956}$

2 $4\frac{3}{7}$ $4\frac{3}{7}$

$+ 2\frac{2}{7}$ $- 2\frac{2}{7}$

3 What value does **X** represent on the number line?

25   50   75

_____

4 Write the correct symbol in the circle.

< = >

$9.46 - 8.41$ $8.49 - 6.82$

5 Beth is sorting her dirty clothes. There are 15 pairs of pants, 12 T-shirts, and 4 sweatshirts. If the washing machine will hold only 4 T-shirts or 2 sweatshirts and 3 pairs of pants at one time, how many loads of laundry will Beth have to do to clean all her clothes?

_____ loads

➤ Activity 1

Use the following clues to determine the whole number that goes in each section of the figure and what color each section should be. Write the correct whole number next to each letter and color the section correctly.

Clues

- The sum of the sections in the oval is 15.
- The sum of the sections in the rectangle is 9.
- The sum of the sections in the triangle is 16.
- The number 5 is in the black section.
- Section F is blue.
- The number 2 is in the green section.
- The intersection of all three shapes is red.
- The number 3 is in section A.
- The section that is **only** in the oval is green.
- Section E is orange.
- One of the sections is yellow.

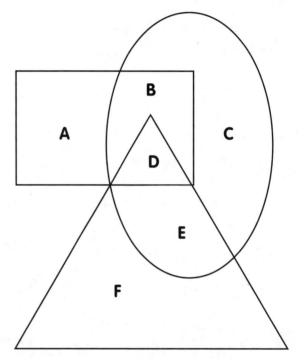

➤ Activity 2

Draw the hands on each clock to show the time. Write the name of the angle that the hands make (**right**, **acute**, or **obtuse**) on the line under the clock.

4:45

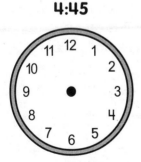

_____

3:00

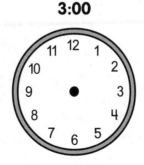

_____

11:55

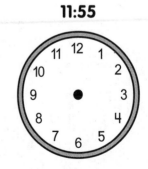

_____

1   Is the equation correct?   **yes   no**
    If **no**, correct any errors.

    $67.29 - 38.5 = 28.79$

2   Is the equation correct?   **yes   no**
    If **no**, correct any errors.

    $\frac{2}{7} + \frac{3}{7} = \frac{5}{14}$

3   Continue the pattern.

    10 17 24 31 _____ _____ _____

    _____ _____ _____ _____

4   How many cups are in one gallon?

    _____ cups

5   Joy and Jo Ellen are baking brownies for their class party. Each batch makes 18 brownies. They want to make enough so that each student can have 2 brownies. If there are 25 students in the class, how many batches of brownies do they need to bake?

    _____ batches

1   $6{,}327 \div 9 =$ _____

2   $\begin{array}{r} 56 \\ \times 48 \\ \hline \end{array}$

3   Find the perimeter.

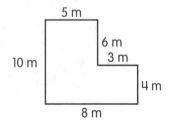

    _____

4   What is the area of the figure in problem 3?

    _____

5   Parker went for a four-hour bike ride on Saturday afternoon. If his average speed was about 8 miles an hour, approximately how many miles did Parker ride?

    _____ miles

1 (3 + 4) x 6 = _____

3 + (4 x 6) = _____

2 Solve for *y*.

$y \div 66 = 42$ y = _____

3 Here are three views of the same cube. Which letter is on the side opposite the **A**?

_____

4 Complete the table.

oz.	lb.
16	1
___	2
48	___
___	___

5 Peyton wants to buy 3 CDs. Each CD costs $14.95. How much will the CDs cost in all?

$_____

1 7)4,515

2 98
 x 57
 ____

3 At which time of day do the hands on a clock form a straight angle?

○ 8:00   ○ 3:00   ○ 6:00

4 What temperature is 18 degrees higher than 78 degrees?

_____ degrees

5 Caleb has 27 cookies. He wants to divide them evenly between himself and his 4 friends. How many whole cookies will each of them get?

_____ cookies

As Camp Kickapoo's activity director, Lisa is in charge of arranging field trips for the campers. It's the end of the season, and Lisa still has $1,000.00 left in her field-trip budget. She wants to use the money to take the campers and counselors to an apiary to see how bees make honey. Use the information below to help Lisa determine the cost of the trip for 51 campers, 8 counselors, and 2 directors.

Apiary ticket prices:
Children: $5.00
Adults: $6.75

Group discount:
1 adult admission free
with every 15 paid tickets

Transportation:
$75.00 per van (1 van
holds 18 passengers)

Refreshments:
$1.50 per person

Work space

Admission:

    Campers $_____

    Adults $_____

Transportation: $_____

Refreshments: $_____

Total cost of trip: $_____

Does Lisa have enough money in the budget?   ○ **yes**   ○ **no**

How to Solve
Word Problems

 Read the problem carefully. Think about what it says.

 Read the problem again and look for clue words. They will tell you which operation to use. Below are some examples of clue words.

 Solve the problem. **Hint:** Sometimes you will use more than one operation.

 Check your work. Does your answer make sense?

Clue Words

Add	Subtract	Multiply	Divide
in all	more than	times	parts
altogether	less than	product of	equal parts
total	are left	multiply by	separated
sum	take away	area	divided by
both	difference	by	quotient of
plus	fewer	(with measurements or dimensions)	a fraction of
			average

Place Value Chart

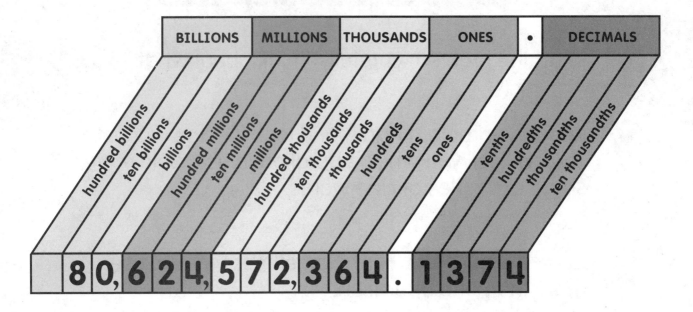

BILLIONS			MILLIONS			THOUSANDS			ONES			.	DECIMALS			
hundred billions	ten billions	billions	hundred millions	ten millions	millions	hundred thousands	ten thousands	thousands	hundreds	tens	ones		tenths	hundredths	thousandths	ten thousandths
8	0,	6	2	4,	5	7	2,	3	6	4		.	1	3	7	4

Metric and Standard Length Chart

Metric	Standard
1 kilometer (km)	0.62 mile (mi.)
1 kilometer (km)	3,280.8 feet (ft.)
1 meter (m)	3.28 feet (ft.)
1 centimeter (cm)	0.39 inch (in.)
1 millimeter (mm)	0.039 inch (in.)
1 inch (in.)	2.54 centimeters (cm)
1 inch (in.)	25.4 millimeters (mm)
1 foot (ft.)	0.30 meter (m)
1 yard (yd.)	0.00091 kilometer (km)
1 mile (mi.)	1.61 kilometers (km)

Congratulations!

_____
(name)

You have successfully
completed your
math practice!